How to Read
Marx's *Capital*

How to Read Theory

Series Editors:
Stephen Shapiro, Department of English and
Comparative Literary Studies, University of Warwick
Ed White, Department of English, University of Florida

'How to Read Theory' is a new series of clear, introductory guides to critical theory and cultural studies classics designed to encourage readers to think independently. Each title focuses on a single, key text and concisely explains its arguments and significance, showing the contemporary relevance of theory and presenting difficult theoretical concepts in clear, jargon-free prose. Presented in a compact, user-friendly format, the 'How to Read Theory' series is designed to appeal to students and to interested readers everywhere who are coming to these key texts for the first time. Never before have the classic texts of theory and cultural studies been made so accessible.

How to Read
Marx's *Capital*

Stephen Shapiro

Pluto Press

LONDON • ANN ARBOR, MI

First published 2008 by Pluto Press
345 Archway Road, London N6 5AA
and 839 Greene Street, Ann Arbor, MI 48106

www.plutobooks.com

British Library Cataloguing in Publication Data
A catalogue record for this book is available from the British Library

ISBN   978 0 7453 2562 0   hardback
ISBN   978 0 7453 2561 3   paperback

Library of Congress Cataloging in Publication Data applied for

10 9 8 7 6 5 4 3 2 1

Designed and produced for Pluto Press by
Chase Publishing Services Ltd, Fortescue, Sidmouth, EX10 9QG, England
Typeset from disk by Stanford DTP Services, Northampton
Printed and bound in India

Contents

Preface   viii

PART ONE: COMMODITIES AND MONEY

1. The Commodity   1
2. The Process of Exchange   40
3. Money, or the Circulation of Commodities   43

PART TWO: THE TRANSFORMATION OF MONEY INTO CAPITAL

4. The General Formula for Capital   55
5. Contradictions in the General Formula   60
6. The Sale and Purchase of Labour-Power   63

PART THREE: THE PRODUCTION OF ABSOLUTE SURPLUS-VALUE

7. The Labour Process and the Valorization Process   72
8. Constant Capital and Variable Capital   78
9. The Rate of Surplus-Value   79
10. The Working Day   82
11. The Rate and Mass of Surplus-Value   92

PART FOUR: THE PRODUCTION OF RELATIVE SURPLUS-VALUE

12. The Concept of Relative Surplus-Value   96
13. Co-operation   98
14. The Division of Labour and Manufacture   105
15. Machinery and Large-Scale Industry   117

PART FIVE: THE PRODUCTION OF ABSOLUTE AND RELATIVE SURPLUS-VALUE

16. Absolute and Relative Surplus-Value   140
17. Changes of Magnitude in the Price of
    Labour-Power and in Surplus-Value   141
18. Different Formulae for the Rate of Surplus-Value   141

PART SIX: WAGES

19. The Transformation of the Value
    (and Respectively the Price) of Labour-Power
    into Wages   142
20. Time-Wages   142
21. Piece-Wages   142
22. National Differences in Wages   142

PART SEVEN: THE PROCESS OF ACCUMULATION OF CAPITAL

23. Simple Reproduction   145
24. The Transformation of Surplus-Value into
    Capital   147
25. The General Law of Capitalist Accumulation   150

PART EIGHT: SO-CALLED PRIMITIVE ['ORIGINATING'] ACCUMULATION

26. The Secret of Primitive Accumulation   159
27. The Expropriation of the Agricultural
    Population from the Land   162
28. Bloody Legislation Against the Expropriated
    Since the End of the Fifteenth Century.
    The Forcing Down of Wages by Act of
    Parliament   166

29. The Genesis of the Capitalist Farmer   167
30. Impact of the Agricultural Revolution on
    Industry. The Creation of a Home Market for
    Industrial Capital   167
31. The Genesis of the Industrial Capitalist   168
32. The Historical Tendency of Capitalist
    Accumulation   171
33. The Modern Theory of Colonization   172

Suggestions for Further Reading   174
Index   176

Preface

For a writer like Marx, who glories in contradictions, here's one: the length and complexity of the first volume of *Capital* pose a daunting challenge to first-time readers. Yet few other works in the modern age have been so important to such a widely international audience, especially those with little formal education or literacy. Marx himself was acutely aware of the tension between the difficulty of *Capital*'s early passages and his desire that the book should be meaningful to the working class. While encouraging readers to persevere, he also, at times, suggested that they might skip the first, more theoretical, parts and asked his life-long collaborator, Friedrich Engels, to summarize *Capital*'s arguments in a shorter book.

What Marx could assume, though, was that his contemporaries would have some familiarity with the terminology and basic outline of his argument, since they belonged to a widespread left-wing culture and community. Today is a different story. Many of you will be reading Marx in isolation from any supportive environment. Even those lucky enough to be in a classroom that discusses Marx will find that the pressures of modern education often do not allow time to see the full panorama of *Capital*'s arguments. You may find that you will be told what Marx claims, but not have the space to process Marx's construction of his claims in ways that allow you to think these through for yourself.

How to Read Marx's Capital attempts to support readers in their early steps towards a self-reliant understanding of Marx. Just as no printed map can replace the personal experience of learning the way to a destination, this book should enable, but not replace, your own reading of *Capital*. No abbreviated version can convey the richness of Marx's writing or even pretend at completeness, but it may, hopefully, give you the confidence to discover these for yourself. To help ease your way, I follow *Capital*'s chapter-by-chapter structure and often quote Marx's own words so they will seem less strange or incomprehensible when you next read them. Ideally this method will equip you to read further in Marx and all those later writers who take his claims as their starting point. In short, this guide should be a starting point, not a conclusion.

There are two standard English translations of the first volume of *Capital* from the German, a nineteenth-century one by Samuel Moore and Edward Aveling and a twentieth-century one by Ben Fowkes, which is easily available in a Penguin Books edition (first published 1976). There are good reasons to prefer either version, but the translation referenced here is Fowkes's. All quotations will be parenthetically indexed to this later edition.

A few words about words. In *Capital*, Marx refers to 'capital' but never to 'capitalism', since the style of 'ism-ing' a social or cultural movement was less common in his day. Here I use 'capital' and 'capitalism' as interchangeable, often preferring the latter as less awkward for contemporary English readers. In his translator's note, Fowkes explains that he renders the German word *Arbeiter* as 'worker', rather than 'labourer', which Moore and Aveling used. Fowkes did so because, in 1976, he felt that 'worker' had less of a negative connotation than 'labourer'. Today, the reverse might be true. Rather than be held hostage to momentary tastes, I use both without prejudice.

One feature of capitalist-defined modernity is that an author, as a producer of text, is distanced from her or his readers, the consumers of that text, by the interference of the price-setting market place. A book, after all, is also a commodity and thus subject to the same rules of capitalist commodification that Marx brilliantly describes in *Capital*. Though we may be anonymous to each other, I do not write in isolation. For the possibility of these pages has been made not only by Marx, but as well by the many who have struggled to achieve a better life than the one that capitalism has on offer. Similarly, my intention is not just that you read this simply to understand Marx, but to use your comprehension to carry on with the unfinished project of repairing the damage that capital has wreaked on human life and aspirations.

Für Anne

Part One: Commodities and Money

Chapter 1. The Commodity

Section 1. The Two Factors of the Commodity: Use-Value and Value (Substance of Value, Magnitude of Value)

Marx begins *Capital* by saying that '[t]he wealth of societies in which the capitalist mode of production prevails appears as an "immense collection of commodities"; the individual commodity appears as its elementary form. Our analysis therefore begins with the analysis of the commodity' (125).

These opening lines contain three interlocking themes – analytical, socio-historical, and experiential – that recur in Marx's study of capitalism. Firstly, he rejects the claims of free-market, 'liberal' economists, typically represented by Adam Smith's 1776 *An Inquiry into the Nature and Causes of the Wealth of Nations*. Even if you have not formally studied any economics, you are probably familiar with the common sense of liberal political economy, because its claims are the ones often taken to be true by mainstream politicians and journalists. Smith argues that market exchanges involve consensual agreements between buyers and sellers, who trade with one another to satisfy their own needs. In this light, he believes that if commerce is liberated from the state's interference through taxes and tariffs, then the market place will spontaneously expand to benefit everyone. For Smith, while humans trade for selfish reasons, they must, however, learn to co-operate with each other to achieve their desires. This produces fellow feeling, which, along with the checks of supply and demand, is the 'invisible hand' that prevents traders from creating market crises and conflict.

By replacing Smith's phrase – 'the wealth of nations' – with 'the wealth of societies', Marx indicates that he intends *Capital* to be, as his subtitle says, 'a critique of political economy'. By using the word 'societies' rather than 'nations', Marx suggests that the basic assumptions of free-marketers are wrong. Our immediate problem involves the structure of capitalist *society* and the way its economic practices create profit, not the relationship between the nation-state and the market place. While Marx later explains the role of governments in assisting the rise of capitalism, he sees it as a structure greater than individual nation-states, even while governments frequently shape its contours through legislation. Marx calls his book a critique, rather than a criticism, of political economy, because he will not just disagree with writers like Smith, he will explain *how* their arguments are wrong in that they are based on partial claims, ones made often without regard to the historical development of market relations, especially in the turn from a feudal to a modern commercial society.

The introductory line's second theme, consequently, is a historical one. With the phrase, 'in which the capitalist mode of production prevails', Marx insists that he is not writing about societies in general. He wants instead to focus specifically on societies in which capitalist economic practices dominate – capitalist societies. Throughout *Capital*, Marx constantly highlights the *particular* features that make capitalism new and distinctive from pre-capitalist practices, even while it also incorporates elements from the past. Marx often begins his chapters by discounting popular definitions of words and replacing them with his own, because he thinks that the commonly used ones obscure (and implicitly justify) the newness of capitalism. This fussiness about definitions may seem pedantic, but Marx does so because he wants his readers to understand why capitalism differs from older kinds of commodity exchanges and labour practices so that we can perceive what needs to be changed to get outside the damaging world that capitalism makes. If we learn what makes capitalism unique and how it *began*, then we can think about how it may *end*. To replace capitalism with a post-capitalist world – no matter what word we use for this: socialism, communism, or any other name – we need to know what specifically turns market trades into capitalist market trades.

The third theme follows on from the first two as it involves how we come to understand capitalism's historical transformation of non-capitalist societies. At first glance, capitalist societies seem to be different, because they create an 'immense collection of commodities'. We do not have to be economic experts to realize that more and more things are for sale than in the past. In the end, Marx will not actually define capitalist societies by their creation of consumer choices. One of Marx's major claims in *Capital* is that different economic practices should always be defined in terms of how and why they *produce* goods, rather than how and why people *consume* them. A basic difference between Marx and liberal economists like Smith rests in this difference of perspective. Smith considers the market place of consumer choices as the only important sphere of economic practices. Marx insists that the sphere of production is the actual location that matters.

At this point in *Capital*, he has not yet made this claim. Why then start by talking about an effect of capitalism, the 'appearance' of consumable commodities, rather than its defining feature of how it produces these commodities? Marx begins in what seems to be the reverse order to illustrate his belief that we have to start with what we experience, what is before our eyes, and then work 'backwards' to learn what causes these effects. Throughout *Capital*, Marx first describes an aspect of capitalism and then explains its cause. Sometimes he delays this explanation for a very long time. For example, Marx waits until the volume's last part, 'So-Called Primitive Accumulation', to explain how capitalism emerged from pre-capitalist societies and what lies at the root of all capitalist accumulation. Why not start with the beginning? After all, one of the most frustrating challenges for first-time readers of *Capital* is that because Marx argues from appearance (the effect) to cause, rather than the reverse, we have to struggle through the first sections of *Capital*, which are notoriously difficult to follow because their dense philosophical language makes it hard to perceive where the argument is leading or why a dry and abstract discussion of value is necessary before turning to the gripping, and almost immediately understandable, description of exploited workers.

Yet the strange thing is that once you have read the entire book and understood its argument, *Capital*'s early pages will in retrospect seem almost obvious. Marx says that this initial difficulty of comprehension is true for every new way of understanding the world. The principle of gravity was once hard to conceptualize, even while we have always experienced its effects, because humans first have to understand that the earth rotates around the sun, and pre-Galilean science thought that the earth was stationary. Nowadays the notion of gravity seems self-evident because we have the analytical tools that make the concept clear. You might find the same happening with your own reading of *Capital*. What seems hard at first becomes easier when you look back and recall Marx's later, concrete examples.

Marx writes in this way, though, to make an additional point. He wants to insist that we can use our everyday experiences as the medium for understanding the world's unseen complexities, and, furthermore, that world revolutions happen when we transform these experiences, rather than simply inventing new abstract, philosophical concepts in isolation from what we perceive. *Capital* is a revolutionary text, not because Marx has realized something before anyone else (although he does claim this); its power results from how Marx gives us a critical language to describe what we already know, even if in a vague and incoherent fashion, and then redirect this new-found understanding through social and political action. Even though Marx was himself well aware that *Capital*'s terms and organization make it challenging to read, he still kept them, even after many drafts and revisions, because he wants to teach us how to think through a problem and not just passively learn his answers. Marx wants to empower his readers by showing us that we can learn how to learn and become engaged in changing society.

Before continuing, one other important feature of this version of *Capital*'s first paragraph is worth mentioning.

All the English versions of *Capital* translate the original German of 'eine "ungeheure Warensammlung"' as 'an "immense collection of commodities"'. While it is not incorrect to use 'immense' for 'ungeheure', the word can also be translated as 'monstrous'. On one hand, 'immense' makes sense because Marx argues that the logic of capitalism results in a massive increase in the number of produced commodities. On the other, 'monstrous' conveys Marx's recurring argument that quantitative, empirically verifiable changes in society become qualitative ones. The manner of capitalist production not only increases the number of commodities, it also fundamentally makes this growth of commodities frightening, not least because the way that commodities are used in capitalist societies has disturbing effects on human life, even beyond the immediate realm of labourers. Within capitalism, commodities appear like monsters, as Marx explains, because they seem to be super-naturally more powerful than humans, partially as a result of the dehumanizing work conditions that capitalism always creates. Throughout *Capital*, Marx uses the language of Gothic horror – vampires, werewolves, dripping blood – to describe capitalism's human costs. Even within *Capital*'s first words, Marx inscribes his ethical outrage at the moral hell that capitalism has unleashed on our life world.

After this opening, Marx says that we must begin our study of capitalism with 'an analysis of the commodity' as its 'elementary' or most basic unit. What is a commodity? A commodity is an outside object, 'a thing which through its qualities satisfies human needs of whatever kind. The nature of these needs, whether they arise, for example, from the stomach, or the imagination, makes no difference' (125). These needs might be physical and necessary for

　　　　　　　　　　How to Read Marx's *Capital*

basic survival (like food) or 'fanciful' (like the desire for pornography). Marx is not interested here in evaluating different kinds of wants. Both vegetables and pornography are 'useful' in the sense that we consume them to satisfy a personal need, be it digestive or erotic. Instead of differentiating between 'good' and 'bad' commodities, Marx says that every useful object can instead be looked at from the viewpoints of 'quality and quantity'. These two factors of material qualities and abstract quantities indicate two different kinds of 'value' that Marx will shortly define as *use-value* and *exchange-value*.

An object can be useful in multiple ways. A shoe might be used to protect feet or it might excite a foot fetishist. The qualitative ways in which these uses alter throughout time is a topic for (cultural) historians, who might want to know why one age prefers wearing boots rather than shoes, for instance. Marx's focus here instead treats how measuring the *quantities* of these objects changes, for this will unravel the nature of capitalism. In short, he will study the history of the production of exchange-values, not use-values, since capitalist societies are ones defined by their search for and production of quantified exchange-values.

Because an object's use-value depends on its material qualities, its 'physical body' (126), an object can be more or less useful depending on how well its natural properties satisfy our needs. If we want to keep warm on a winter's night, a wool coat is more useful than a nylon one, but if we want to keep dry on a wet summer one, then a nylon windbreaker is more useful than a heavy winter jacket that weighs us down because its wool absorbs water. Because 'the usefulness of a thing makes it a use-value', an object's utility can only be 'realized in the use or in consumption'

(126), rather than as an abstract number. We might decide to rate a coat's relative comfort on a scale of 1 to 10, but we would recognize the relative arbitrariness, if not silliness, of these numbers. Furthermore, a coat is useful only when we actually wear it; we cannot make the quality of warmth real to us ('realizable') if it sits on the shelf. So use-value comes from using an object. Yet while an object's 'material wealth' – its material softness, warmth, etc. – determines its usefulness (what Marx calls its utility), 'in the form of society to be considered here' (i.e. a capitalist one), commodities 'are also the material bearers of . . . exchange-value' (126).

Exchange-value is harder to perceive and experience than use-value because it depends on intangible, numerical (quantitative) aspects, involving how much it can be traded for in exchange for other commodities. We can realize a commodity's use-value by personally consuming it, but its 'exchange-value' appears only when we try to sell it and see if anyone else will pay to use or consume it. Until someone else agrees to buy an object, it does not really have an exchange-value. We might collect old comic books, which might have a use-value to us, even if only a sentimental or nostalgic one. The comics might also have an exchange-value, but we do not know how much or little that may be until we try putting them up for sale or watch what happens when someone else does so.

Because a commodity's exchange-value is not determined by human satisfaction, it only emerges in the market place. An ornately carved chair and a rough stool might have, more or less, the same use-value, the usefulness of lifting us off the ground, but when selling the two, we discover that the delicately crafted chair has a greater exchange-value. We cannot know that one chair has a larger exchange-value by sitting on it; this information emerges only when the two chairs are brought to the market to be sold. Exchange-value, thus, is registered in the absence of sensuous satisfaction; it is an 'abstract' feature and as such requires an imaginary standard of measurement. This lack of personal immediacy makes exchange-value a feature that seems to be both outside of the object, as it refers to this standard, and within it, given that it does not relate to human utility.

There is a contradiction here. How can an object's exchange-value be simultaneously extrinsic and relative, since it depends on the 'accident' of how much others might pay us for it in the market, and yet seemingly intrinsic, or belonging to the chair, given that it has a quality that does not depend on human needs for use?

Before we try to solve this riddle, notice how Marx constructs his arguments. He frequently pursues a question until it seems to reach a contradiction. At this point, he uses this paradox to carry his exploration further. It often seems as if Marx assumes that finding a contradiction means that he is coming closer to the point where a solution can be found, rather than a sign that his argument has gone wrong and come to a dead end. He looks for contradictions because he thinks that these will discover the weak point in our understanding, the terms that need revising because their current use has become untenable. When Marx's commentators talk about his 'dialectical' style of argument, they mean how he looks for paradoxes to redefine his terms and argument. The search for contradictions between two elements that reshape an initial problem consistently features in *Capital* as the logic that structures the flow of Marx's argument. Marx often seems to zigzag back to alter earlier points to show how our initial perceptions can be refined in light of later realizations.

To return to our discussion, the outside/inside problem can be answered by recognizing that exchange-value depends on our ability to find something that both characterizes the commodity apart from our use of it and acts as a means for it to be equated with other commodities. If I have corn and want to trade it for iron, to satisfy my need for raw material to forge a plough, how much corn do I need to offer in return for a certain amount of iron? Because corn and iron are materially different substances and have very different use-values, there needs to be something against which they can be compared, or made equivalent, so that I know to trade my corn's exchange-value for a proper amount of the iron's exchange-value. This standard of measure 'cannot be a geometrical, physical, chemical or other natural property of the commodities' (127), because these material features belong to an object's use-value, and we need something intangible, something different from a commodity's useful, physical substance, to determine its exchange-value. An 'exchange-value cannot be anything other than the mode of expression, the "form of appearance", of a content distinguishable from it' (127). This 'appearance-form' is 'characterized precisely by its abstraction', it is a conceptual (or 'idealized') aspect that belongs neither to the commodity's natural properties, nor to its use-value to humans. Unlike use-value, which has a tangible effect, exchange-value is simply a form of expression, a marker or sign for something else, which does not belong to the commodity's physical nature. For instance, a numeral like the number '5' does not have any use-value, it does not have any concrete 'fiveness'. 'Fiveness' belongs to the collection of five actual objects, let's say apples. The number '5' is only a conceptual device, an abstract marker that erases the concrete differences between the individual apples, such as their particular shape, colour, or taste.

Just as written numerals are used to relate numbers to one another and then process them in equations – we add, subtract, multiply, or divide numbers – similarly, exchange-values, unlike use-values, exist to facilitate the process of transfers – the market place's exchange. Once we have consumed an object, we have 'used' it up, and it stops having a use-value because it literally no longer exists. But a commodity's exchange-value has a 'phantom-like objectivity' (128) that hovers alongside the object as it passes from hand to hand in different exchanges, much like a ghost gliding next to human bodies. What creates this spectral effect of a commodity's exchange-value?

If exchange-value does 'not contain an atom of use-value', and use-value depends on the object's material presence, then 'only one property remains' outside of the object's physical features: the human labour that has been put into making an object. An object has exchange-value 'only because human labour is objectified or materialized in it' (129). The source of all value is human labour.

When we make an object, we transfer the energy from our activity (what Marx calls our 'unrest') into a fixed object. This is to say that labour-created value has been 'objectified' when it moves from an impermanent, human subject to a fixed, material object, much as when the energy of flowing water congeals to form a static cube of ice. This displaced labour is the latent force that generates the commodity's use- and exchange-values. Human labour works on nature to make it useful, as when a carpenter planes wood to make a chair. The labour that the carpenter invests in making the chair also gives it an exchange-value that is accidental and relative, since not every substance will get the carpenter's interest, as well as seemingly intrinsic to the chair, because our senses cannot register the work that has gone into the chair. We can feel the chair's smooth texture, but not the labour that went into producing this sensation. Exchange-value is ghostly because it is the incorporeal residue of labour that is always connected to an object, even though it cannot be grasped, smelt, or otherwise registered by our senses. For this reason, exchange-value has to be given a 'form' or medium which it can inhabit to make it 'appear' to us, just as a cartoonist will throw a bedsheet over a ghost to make it visible.

The claim that human labour is the 'substance' of value is known, unsurprisingly, as the 'labour theory of value', and it is absolutely basic to Marx's argument in *Capital*. Whenever you become uncertain as to what Marx is arguing in a passage, keep this claim as your lodestone.

If human labour is the 'value-forming substance', it can be numerically measured by the amount of labour-time spent on making an object. The *magnitude* (or size) of any object's value is simply a representation of 'the labour-time socially necessary for its production' (129).

If the quantity of human labour determines the degree of a commodity's value, does an object become more valuable if a lazy person spends a longer time making a chair than a more industrious one? No. 'What exclusively determines the magnitude of the value of an article is therefore the amount of labour socially necessary, or the labour-time socially necessary for its production' (129).

Marx says that he is concerned only with the 'socially average' amount of time required to produce a commodity 'under the conditions of production normal for a given society and with the average degree of skill and intensity prevalent in that society' (129). If a commodity can be generally made in one hour, then the value I spend on making it is equal to one hour, even if I personally take longer to make it. This average is not based on an individual's qualities, but is an abstraction, an average quantity of many workers.

Here we are beginning to perceive another difference between use-value and exchange-value. A commodity's usefulness is generally determined in a non-numerical way, based on our needs, which are difficult to quantify, especially as they are often highly idiosyncratic. As the calculation of a commodity's exchange-value is based on the average amount of labour-time that it takes to make it, this social average ignores individual skills and differences to treat human labour as an abstraction, a force that can almost be considered separate from humans themselves. Exchange-value depersonalizes human energy and creativity as it relies on inanimate numbers.

A commodity's value changes (or is 'relative') due to a number of factors: the average skill level of workers, the technical sophistication of the equipment used to make a commodity, the social organization of the work process, its efficiency, and the prevalence of raw materials in nature. Here Marx foreshadows a point he will later take up in Chapter 15, 'Machinery and Large-Scale Industry', when he says that new technologies can cheapen a commodity and lower its value as they reduce the average amount of time spent to make something. A handloom weaver might be very fast, but the introduction of a machine-driven power loom radically changes the average time needed to make a piece of clothing. This reduction of the time diminishes its value and consequently the cost of the labour necessary to make the commodity. 'The value of a commodity' thus varies inversely with the productivity of labour, or the amount of time necessary to produce the commodity. The less labour-time it takes to make a commodity, the less value that commodity has contained ('crystallized') within it.

Natural seasons or disasters can also change a commodity's exchange-value. A bushel of corn picked when corn is in season has less value than one picked out of season, because the prevalence of corn makes it easier to find and harvest a bushel. Diamonds are valuable because they are difficult to find and require a tremendous amount of labour to mine, not because of any received sense of their beauty. If it were easy to create diamonds through some new scientific process, such as by 'transforming carbon into diamonds' without 'much labour', then 'their value might fall below that of bricks' (130–1). We might find that diamonds suddenly 'look' less pretty or 'cheaper' to us (as we often say about zirconium substitutes) if they require less work to produce. This may suggest that our aesthetic appreciation is a feature of human productivity rather than of any 'natural beauty'.

We now know that the *substance* of value is labour and *the measure of its magnitude* is labour-time. Yet if these are our working definitions, what really differentiates use-value from exchange-value? Surely both require labour? To overcome this problem, Marx argues that we still need to define the *form* through which abstract labour gets expressed in order to perceive exchange-value's difference from use-value.

To do this, Marx revises his earlier definition of a commodity. Previously he had defined the source of a commodity's use-value as its combination of natural materials and labour. Marx now separates these and explains that 'a thing can be a use-value without being a value' (131). We might find nature useful to us as it provides life-sustaining light, water, and unplanted, food-bearing meadows and forests. Yet because no human labour went into providing these useful objects, they have no labour-created 'value'. (Today we might argue that because our ecology is subjected to human labour, such as when water becomes purified, nature does indeed have a labour-inflected value. But for the purposes of his argument, Marx adopts the more basic claim here that nature provides certain of its resources freely.)

Additionally, a person who produces objects that satisfy her or his own interests, but are not useful to others, does not create 'social use-values'. I might spend a lot of time and effort making a ball out of rubber bands, but this probably only satisfies my own amusement needs, not anyone else's. 'If a thing is useless [to someone other than its creator], so is the labour contained in it; the labour does not count as labour, and therefore has no value' (131). Consequently, 'nothing can be a value without being an object of utility' (131). A commodity must have a social, not personal, use-value for it then to have an exchange-value.

Yet by revising his definition of a commodity to be an object created to satisfy another's use needs through the act of exchange, Marx seems to be further confusing matters by introducing a chicken-and-egg contradiction. He insists that an object's 'social' exchangeability must exist before it can be considered as having a use-value, even while a commodity's use-value must precede its exchange (there's no point in trying to sell something useless). Realizing the muddle that he seems to have created, Marx knows that he must find another way to differentiate use-value from exchange-value. If there are two kinds of value, both of which come from the same source (labour), then there must be a way to differentiate between two kinds of labour, each leading, as the next section's title indicates, to a different kind of value. Before we see what is the dual character of labour embodied in commodities, notice how Marx's argument has shifted. He has moved us from looking at what first appeared to be the basic unit of capitalism, the consumed commodity, and made us more aware of human labour as the underlying ('elemental') source of a commodity's value.

Section 2. The Dual Character of the Labour Embodied in Commodities

We initially saw that a commodity has a twofold character of value, its use-value and its exchange-value. We can now recognize that the labour going into the commodity's production also has a dual character, since the labour for use-value is not recognized in the same way as the labour for exchange-value.

Because use-values are qualitative effects, two similarly usable objects cannot be immediately exchanged as commodities. A coat has a use-value; it satisfies a particular want: our need to keep warm. If we only consider use-values, it would be silly to exchange one coat for another, since at the level of needs, we just want to have any coat that keeps us warm, assuming that all the coats are more or less the same. Objects only become tradable commodities when they satisfy entirely different needs.

Linen, for example, is a commodity that can be used to satisfy various kinds of use; it might be made into a man's coat or a woman's dress. Because different uses can emerge from the same material, there are different kinds of useful labour that can be performed on that material; the labour of a tailor to make a coat is unlike that of a dressmaker. If exchange depends on the trading of different objects to satisfy different needs, there has to be an underlying 'social division of labour' (132) that separates the production of a coat from that of a dress, to continue with our example.

Yet while a 'division of labour is a necessary condition for commodity production', Marx cautions that merely because a division of labour exists, it does not necessarily mean that 'commodities' are produced. 'Simple' village communities might divide labour roles between the women, who cook and sew, and the men, who hunt and gather. In this cohesive unit, all the women and men have a shared need for food and clothing. The community has merely divided labour tasks in order to facilitate everyone's use of the produced objects. Without this separation of use needs, there is no need for the goods to be exchanged through a market place that requires exchange-value's quantitative medium. An object becomes a commodity only when one coherent group (or individual) produces objects to exchange with an extramural coherent group (or individual), where these players, unlike and somewhat isolated from each other, have heterogeneous needs that have to be satisfied. The division of labour in a village between men and women does not create a market for trade between buyers and sellers who only know that the other has something to exchange, not what use needs they must have that compel them to exchange. The men and the women redistribute the food and clothing that each has made directly, without consideration of the labour that went into each occupation, because they recognize their interdependence and that everyone in the group needs these useful objects regardless of the time necessary to make them.

Exchange-value thus arises from increased social complexity and relative loss of shared relationships, which are replaced by a connection to an increasingly anonymous, impersonal mediating sphere, the market place. As groups increasingly relate directly to the market and only indirectly to other groups, this dislocation results in the increased focus on exchange-value as the 'form' of value that allows them to trade dissimilar objects in order to satisfy dissimilar use needs.

Before we move on, it is important to note that Marx does not condemn commodity production, in the sense of creating an object that is traded to satisfy someone else's needs and in return for an object that satisfies the needs of the producers. Indeed, he thinks that such a chain of production and consumption is 'a condition of human existence which is independent of all forms of society; it is an eternal natural necessity' (133). Once we have moved beyond very basic, self-sufficient village groups, commodity production is the human condition.

Marx introduces the consideration of social exchange not to criticize it in general, but as the key to understanding what happens within capitalist societies. He takes us from 'the commodity as an object of utility to the value of commodities' (134) because capitalism is defined by its constant, if not obsessive, production of commodities to accumulate exchange-values, rather than to satisfy use-values. The notion that commodities have dual values, a use-value and an exchange-value, forms a large part of Marx's difference from Smith, who defines market-place activity as the flows of mutually satisfying trade, the transfer of utility between buyer and seller. Marx argues that while these kinds of mutually satisfying reciprocal trades of use-value can occur, they are not the *dominant* form of trade in capitalist societies, which look to the transfer of exchange-values. Therefore, Smith's overly idealized and somewhat mythical image of the market is wholly insufficient for understanding the modern world.

Notice that within his discussion about the division of labour, Marx has once more shifted his definition of a commodity to being something that can be written as

commodity = use-value + exchange-value.

If labour is the substance of value, then both use-value and exchange-value are derived from labour that has been objectified in commodities. Yet every commodity's use-value emerges from 'productive activity of a definite kind, carried on with a definite aim' (132–3), like making a coat to keep someone else warm. A seller of commodities is solely concerned with the commodity's exchange-value, which can only be measured by the labour-time required to produce it. Two commodities of different qualities and use-values can be exchanged through an expression of the labour-time that went into making them, as the magnitude of one commodity's value is numerically compared to that of the other's. In this shift of focus from use-value to exchange-value, we moved from 'the "how" and the "what" of labour' to 'the "how much", ... the temporal duration of labour' (136).

Marx here momentarily delays his discussion to address a hypothetical concern about using labour-time as the standard. For surely some types of workers' time are more valuable than others. For instance, an hour of a surgeon's labour costs more than an hour of a manual labourer, but only because more labour (i.e. training time) went into educating the surgeon, paying for the support staff aiding her or him, and creating the equipment that she or he uses. Because Marx wants here to simplify an already complex matter for his readers, he temporarily puts aside the question of skilled versus unskilled labour and will 'henceforth view every form of labour-power ... as simple labour-power' (135) and assume the 'simple average of labour' (135) in his considerations. He later returns to the matter of training elite workers, since access to education will be an important site of struggle between labourers and capitalists. In any case, because the

> various proportions in which different kinds of labour are reduced to simple labour as their unit of measurement are established by a social process that goes on behind the backs of the producers, these proportions therefore appear to the producers to have been handed down by tradition. (135)

While Marx does not explore here how certain jobs get more valued than others, he emphasizes that we often fail to recognize that these evaluations are historically determined rather than the way things have always been.

After this digression, Marx returns to the separation of use-value from exchange-value. The social division of labour means that labour, as the source of value, must have a similar duality that corresponds to the commodity's twofold nature. Useful labour involves work that creates use-values. The other aspect of labour is what we might momentarily call exchangeable labour (Marx does not provide this term, but we can imply it from the paralleling structure of his argument), which is labour that creates exchange-value; it is the excess labour designed to be exchanged through a formal medium used to represent abstract labour (labour that is not used to satisfy concrete human needs). Marx, in a later footnote, draws on a distinction that the English language provides to help characterize the difference. 'Labour which creates use-values and is qualitatively determined is called "work" as opposed to "labour"; labour which creates value and is measured quantitatively is called "labour", as opposed to "work"' (138).

The presence of (exchange-)labour highlights the three aspects of value. Two of these – the substance of value (labour) and the magnitude of value (labour-time) – we already recognize as present in both use-value and exchange-value. The difference between these two kinds of value lies with their forms. The form of use-value is the physical quality of the commodity. The form of exchange-value is a 'non-useful' form, within which labour is expressed. Marx turns to explore the nature of this value-form in the next section.

Before moving on, we should recognize that Marx has silently, but significantly, begun to make a distinction that he continues to make from this point on throughout the volume. Having said that use-values cannot be quantified, since they are by definition qualitative factors, Marx increasingly drops use-values out of the discussion. From here on, when he uses the word 'value', he really means exchange-value and when he wants to refer to use-value, he often instead writes 'material wealth' (136) to highlight the material aspect of use, rather than the abstract feature of exchange.

It might also be useful to chart some of Marx's oppositions.

Quality	Quantity
Use-value	Exchange-value
Concrete, sensuous	Abstract, numerical
Natural-form	Value-form (138), Commodity-value (128)
Worth	Value (126)
Material wealth	Magnitude of value (136–7)
Work	Labour (more properly, labour-power) (138)

Section 3. The Value-Form, or Exchange-Value

Marx begins this section on the form of value with another contradiction. Commodities are originally created to satisfy use-values, but they can only be defined as commodities within exchange, where they have a dual nature as 'objects of utility and bearers of [exchange-]value' (138). Since exchange-value has nothing to do with usefulness, Marx argues that commodities have an 'objective character' when they are not considered in terms of human (subjective) satisfaction. In order for us to evaluate the objective form of different kinds of commodities, we need a means of comparing them through an expression of 'an identical social substance' (138).

How to Read Marx's *Capital*

We already know that this social substance is labour, but we do not yet know the form in which it will appear within the market place. Here Marx explains that this 'common value-form' is money. Money is the form through which human labour is quantified. In this section, Marx shows the process that led to the emergence of the money-form as a means of relating 'the values of two commodities'. In what feels like an overly technical discussion, he traces four historical forms of value, because he wants us to see economic forms as transformable historical developments so that we do not assume that the currently dominant form is the only one possible.

The first form of value is 'the simple, isolated, or accidental form of value' (139). This form is close to barter, or direct exchange, as one commodity is simply judged to be equal to a certain amount of another: e.g. 1 coat is worth 2 bolts of linen. This kind of trading makes one commodity (the coat) 'relative' or dependent on the 'equivalent' form of another (linen). A fixed amount of linen is taken to have the same value as a relative number of coats.

For Marx, using one commodity to be the standard of equivalence to another is problematic in two ways. Firstly, the 'relative' form (of notation) masks actual differences (of use and its underlying divisions of labour) between commodities through what may appear to be similarities. Here Marx draws on an example from organic chemistry. In chemistry, one substance might have a certain ratio of common elements, let us say 4 carbon to 8 hydrogen to 2 oxygen atoms. Yet the number of elements within a compound does not determine the effect created by their configuration. Both butyric acid and propyl formate (141) can be written in the same way – $C_4H_8O_2$ – so as to make them seem 'relatively' equal, but in reality they act very differently, because the shape of their 'physical formation' makes them very unlike each other.

Marx uses the scientific metaphor to suggest that using one commodity 'accidentally' to judge another is too imprecise and slippery. Our assumption that 1 coat = 20 yards of cotton is ruined if the value of either of these commodities changes. If there is a poor crop, then it takes more time and labour to get the material to make 20 yards of cotton, meaning that as the value of the cotton increases, then one coat will be traded for less of it. Since the ratio between these commodities can be altered so easily, the equation does not function as well as a long-lasting standard. We have not really got to the source of how commodities are made abstract and equal to one another. So rather than think of cotton and coats 'relatively', we need to find some 'equivalent' that both cotton and coats can be compared to, something more stable that can represent value over time.

The second, and more important, problem with the simple form of value is that if we say that 'commodities are simply congealed quantities of human labour' (141), we entirely reduce them to an 'abstract value'. It would be wrong to make one commodity the standard on which all others are judged, since commodities do have natural, physical forms that satisfy use needs. We could make a mass of sugar the equivalent to which all other commodities are compared, but this would be to forget that sugar is also desirable because we like to use it to sweeten our food. Because sugar has a real use in satisfying certain desires, its exchange-value will vanish if we suddenly decided to consume its use-value by eating it. We cannot ignore the fact that the use-value of certain commodities overwhelms any attempt to make them function as purely abstract forms.

For a commodity to be the 'mirror of value' (150), it must be able to express the abstract quality of human labour, not its material utility. The equivalent form must be a 'social form' that simultaneously transfers value and 'conceals a social relation' (149) involving the division of labour that produces objects. Therefore, an ideal form of exchange-value needs to reduce its utility to as little as possible, otherwise it cannot act as a stable form of equivalence.

Marx summarizes the contradiction between the forms of (exchange-)value and use-value in this way:

> Human labour-power in its fluid state, or human labour, creates value, but is not itself value. It becomes value in its coagulated state, in objective form. The value of the linen as a congealed mass of human labour can be expressed only as an 'objectivity', a thing which is materially different from the linen and yet common to the linen and all other commodities. (142)

What does he mean when he says that human labour-power creates value, but is not value?

One way to think about this riddle would be to replace the word 'value' with something like 'electricity'. Think for a moment about electricity. We know that electrical power can be made using human labour, by burning coal to make steam, for instance; but we cannot really 'hold on' to electricity or recognize its power unless it is made to do something 'through' an object. We only really know that an outlet provides so many volts, and that when we connect it to an appliance that requires a certain amount of energy to operate, it then runs. Electricity provides a use for us, but only if it goes through a medium that calibrates its power between the outlet and the appliance. Similarly, electrical power does not have a 'natural' look to it (what's the colour or texture of electricity?), so we have to make an abstract sign to represent it, often a jagged line with an arrow that looks like a lightning bolt. Using electricity as our example, we can say that while humans create its power, this power can only be recognized at the moment when it works within the form of a non-human object (this is what Marx means when he says value is congealed into a commodity).

Because value is more easily recognizable when it is 'within' the circuit of commodity exchanges, it appears to 'matter' more in that context than when it is outside of exchange (as when it is consumed to satisfy a use or need). Marx uses a helpful metaphor to convey how we often mistake a symbolic form, rather than human relations, as the origin of social energies and values. He makes the point that some men are considered superior to others when they are wearing a general's uniform. We recognize one man as greater in importance when he is wrapped (or, to use Marx's words, 'congealed') within clothes that symbolize power. In this way, the military uniform is a 'bearer of value' (143), even when it has not actually created that value. Human society has created value when it has promoted one man over others and decided that a general should be saluted. The uniform does not actually make a general more important, society does; the coat is only a medium that 'bears' or presents value in an objective form. The value of hierarchy resides in the social institution that decides who gets to wear the uniform legitimately, not simply with the wearing of the uniform. Yet while the military uniform by itself does

How to Read Marx's *Capital*

not make the general more important, the general also needs the uniform so that he can be seen to have greater authority than a private or a civilian. The coat carries value that it does not make; yet this value cannot be expressed without the coat. In modern armies, this point is emphasized as both officers and enlisted soldiers wear the same uniform. A general's coat is not warmer or more durable than a private's. The differences between the uniforms do not lie in their relative use-value, but only in their non-useful insignia, which indicate the wearers' ranks and allow us to compare their 'value-relations' against one another.

Marx now makes what seems to be a tangential comment about the relationship between ideas and social formation, as he claims that the dominant mode of production in every society makes certain intellectual realizations more or less likely. Marx argues that while Aristotle was able to recognize that exchange must have equivalences, he was not able to perceive that these equivalences are based on human labour, because he lived in a society that relied mainly on slave labour. Because Athenian society did not consider all humans as equal, they could not recognize that human labour is the standard of value. Aristotle could not resolve the problem of the twofold nature of the commodity and labour, since he lived in an age that did not provide the social conditions of experience necessary to solve the problem. The 'historical limitation inherent in the society in which he lived prevented him from finding out what "in reality" this relation of equality consisted of' (152).

The significance of Marx's claim that we reach our limits of cognition based on the dominant forms of the society in which we live is twofold. Firstly, Marx implies that it is very difficult to analyse society until we can look back on its operations. Marx was able to critique capitalist activity only because capitalism had already become dominant in modern society. Secondly, the political significance of the claim that thought is conditioned by the historical conditions of its subjects suggests that it will only be possible to understand the problems of a post-capitalist society, a communist one, when that kind of society has emerged. For this reason, perhaps, Marx actually spent little time writing about the details of how a communist society would operate, even though he expected one to arise. Rather than engaging in utopian speculations, the best we can do is to sharpen our clarity as to what defines the features of our current moment, so that we will know what needs to be changed.

After this comment on the historicity of perception, Marx now returns to his main argument on value to confess that when he earlier said that a commodity 'is both a use-value and an exchange-value . . . this was, strictly speaking, wrong' (152). A commodity is an exchanged object of utility (with a use-value) and it has a 'value' (an exchange-value), but only when this value is represented through an abstract representation that is 'distinct from its natural form' and 'in a value-relation or an exchange relation with a second commodity of a different kind' (152). A commodity manifests its exchange-value only when there is a form that can represent or express it against another commodity.

For Marx, this was the mistake that earlier economists made. Both the eighteenth-century Mercantilists, who felt that states ought to hoard gold and raise tariffs, and their opponents, the advocates of free trade, believed in the 'quantitative side of the relative form of value', by which he means that they mistakenly took the 'daily list of prices current on the Stock Exchange' (153) actually to *be* value, rather than simply to *represent* the value created by human labour. They considered the market place to be a sphere of exchange that trades values, rather than a sphere that trades in the *signs of value*, a notation of labour that is transferred into an object.

The problem with the simple form of value is that by making one commodity relative to another, we make one commodity represent use-value (since that is what makes it valuable in the first place) and the other represent exchange-value (as it stands in relation to the other commodity). This is illogical: these two different modes of operation cannot 'speak' to one another, since use-values lack the form of expression that exchange-values have. One commodity's exchange-value makes sense only when expressed in the form of another exchange-value. There is a relationship between use-value and exchange-value, but it cannot be understood with the 'simple form of value' (153), which is just a starting point, an 'embryonic form that must undergo a series of metamorphoses before it can ripen into the price-form' (154). The next step of the sequence is trying to find a solution which will be the turn to the 'total or expanded form of value' (154).

The expanded form of value is the logical consequence of the simple form's equation of one commodity with another. Once we have made one commodity act relative to another, then there is no reason why this process cannot be expanded by adding more relations. For instance, if a certain amount of cotton equals a certain number of coats, then we can add onto this equation by saying that a certain amount of tea equals that magnitude of cotton or coats. If we do so, then we see how commodities can become increasingly compared with many other commodities, as they become 'citizens' of the 'whole world of commodities' (155).

The 'defects' of the expanded form of value are threefold. Firstly, it never expresses the source of value, since it creates an endless series of equivalences; the series of comparisons could be extended without end. 'The chain, of which each equation of value is a link, is liable at any moment to be lengthened by newly created commodities, which will provide the material for a fresh expression of value' (157). By linking too many different kinds of commodities to each other, the chain might wrap around to close into a circle, like a snake swallowing its own tail. If everything becomes equivalent to everything else, we will be unable to find the origin of value.

We might try to get out of this infinite loop by choosing one commodity to be the absolute equivalent to others, for instance, by making every commodity relative to a certain amount of linen. Marx calls this third form the 'general form of value' because one commodity is 'common to all' others (hence it is the general form). Yet Marx sees it as returning to the simple form of value described above, only to repeat the same problem over again, except this time with more commodities. Additionally, it takes one specific kind of labour as the equivalent for all others. If everything is compared to linen, then the weaver's labour is made to be the standard for everything else. This is unsatisfactory because as technology changes the labour-time of weaving, it cannot really operate as the permanent standard of value.

Nonetheless, Marx does see the general form as leading ultimately to the money-form, where one commodity, often gold, becomes the equivalent to other commodities in the form of money. Although gold or silver can have a use-value, as money it is almost wholly used to represent numeric value. Once we see money as the last stage of the development through the simple or accidental, the expanded, and then the general forms, we have solved the problem of how use-value and exchange-value can be connected and expressed, and yet remain separate aspects. Labour creates both use- and exchange-values. Yet the form of use-value lies with its material effects (its usefulness). The form of exchange-value is the money-form's abstract device of equating commodities to each other. This means that we can now rewrite the equation

$$\text{commodity} = \text{use-value} + \text{exchange-value}$$

as

$$\text{commodity} = \text{use-value} + \text{money}.$$

From the perspective of a capitalist, who is interested only in the *form* of value (exchange-value), rather than its *substance* (use-value), the equation appears to be simply

$$\text{commodity} = \text{money},$$

where money lists the commodity's *price*. Having suggested that money is how commodities are 'seen' in capitalist societies, Marx turns in the next section to reviewing the social and cultural implications of commodities' appearance within capitalist societies. Recall *Capital*'s opening lines, since Marx will now explain why commodities seem monstrous in capitalism.

Section 4. The Fetishism of the Commodity and its Secret

With its discussion of commodity fetishism, this section is one of *Capital*'s most frequently read in contemporary cultural studies, as it captures how we experience life in capitalist society, before coming to an awareness of its operations. Marx describes the social psychology that results when commodities are seen from the market place's vantage point of exchange. Returning to the spirit of this part's opening, Marx says that while a commodity is 'an extremely obvious, trivial thing . . . its analysis brings out that it is a very strange thing' (163). When we consider an object for its use-value, there's nothing 'mysterious' about it: we are often familiar with those with whom we trade and understand what needs the object serves, especially if there is a transparent division of labour. But when an object enters the sphere of exchange to become a commodity valued by money in the form of exchange-value, it appears increasingly magical and with a will of its own, like a dancing table or the animated dolls that cartoons often show. The commodity's mystical power, 'clearly, . . . arises from [its] form', but not its physical form, the way in which its material was shaped by labour (the substance of value). Instead, the aura comes from what Marx earlier said was 'the *form*, which stamps *value* as *exchange-value*' (131). Useful objects become commodities through a social division of labour, in which individuals make things in isolation and 'do not come into social contact until they exchange the products of labour' (165). Yet when the sphere of exchange 'mediates' society for us, then the market place's commodities become the only medium in which we see the result of all the accumulated divisions of labour and human relations of production and distribution. Because 'direct social relations between persons in their work' (166) disappear from our gaze in our attempt to understand the world, we are left to see only 'social relations between things' (166), relations which exist 'apart from and outside the producers' (165). Here we seem to have entered a weird world of living commodities, rather than a society of humans. In the world of commodities created for exchange-value, 'the mysterious character of the commodity-form consists therefore simply in the fact that the commodity represents the social characteristics of men's own labour as objective characteristics of the products of labour themselves, as the socio-natural properties of these things' (164–5).

Because commodities are traded as exchange-values, the ways human producers of commodities perceive their own work changes in ways corresponding to use- and exchange-values. Rather than understanding that our labour produces things that are desired to satisfy others' needs, we mainly see commodities within the terms of exchange-value's abstract money-form, and this makes it difficult to see the human source of value. '[Exchange-]value . . . does not have its description branded on its forehead; it rather transforms every product of labour into a social hieroglyphic' that humans must decipher. We approach commodities as if they were like a difficult-to-decode rune, wondering what absent force created them, since we are estranged from our own experience in doing so.

As capitalist commodity exchange alienates human subjects from our own sense of having created commodities, we encounter commodities only in terms of their exchange-value. Yet since this exchange-value is intangible, because we cannot use, eat, or wear it, we are led to believe that things have a life of their own that gives them value beyond whatever use humans might have for them. We mistakenly believe that the object has the power to make itself and communicate with other commodities through the language of prices. As 'sociable' subjects, commodities seem to be exchanging themselves in the market, while humans only seem to be the carriers or 'bearers' of value, like waiters bringing food to the table, not its producers or consumers. Marx characterizes this belief in the power of commodities, rather than human labour-power, as similar to the belief in fetishes, the objects worn close to or as symbolic substitutes for the body, which are believed to have an occult power over us. As we attribute a supernatural power or divine presence to the 'products of men's hands', as if these things could save us from danger or deliver happiness, commodity fetishism is our belief that commodities have power to make us, rather than the other way around. One example of this reversal might be when we believe that new clothing will make us seem sexy, because the clothes, rather than the person wearing them, are perceived to be the origin of sexual attractiveness. Rather than us enlivening the material, the material seems to lend its magic to us. As we become alienated from a sense of control over goods, the commodity instead seems to have become a supernatural force greater than humans. Commodities appear weird, ghostly, and monstrous to us because we sense the presence of the social energy (value) within the commodity, but do not recognize this power as objectified human labour. Our disconnection from the human source of value in the commodity makes it seem uncannily alien.

Commodity fetishism is not (strongly) present in all societies or at all moments in history; it only becomes dominant under the 'peculiar' form of labour relations under capitalism. Since the presence of exchange-value in a commodity comes about very early in human history, as soon as groups begin to trade with one another, and given that an effect of exchange-value is the ghostly form of abstracted labour, then why does Marx argue that the commodity fetish is a defining feature of capitalism? His answer is that a certain threshold has been crossed as capitalism becomes dominant and able to erase our swiftly vanishing sense of a commodity's original site of production. Traders have always cared about how much 'of some other product they get for their own; in what proportions can the products be exchanged?' Yet with the massive increase and repetition of trade, where 'these proportions [of prices] have attained a certain customary stability, they appear to result from the nature of the products' (167). As the price appears to be the true nature of a commodity, rather than its weight or colour, for instance, then it has become fetishized. Commodity fetishism is so common in capitalist societies because these are the ones that massively focus on market-place exchange in ways that vastly amplify commercial attitudes and make them seem to be the origin of value.

Marx then says something that is, on the surface, paradoxical. He argues that understanding '[exchange-]values' as 'merely the material expressions of the human labour expended to produce them . . . marks an epoch in the history of mankind's development, but by no means banishes' the effects of the division (167). Think back to his earlier comments on Aristotle. Understanding the effects of capitalist societies through an investigation into their fundamentals is a modern achievement, which is only possible now that capitalist practices have become easier to recognize, since they have become the main ones. It takes time to recognize the patterns of what might have initially seemed to be 'accidental and ever-fluctuating exchange relations'. The power of habit and repeated custom, however, makes us forget the historical difference of the current moment from the past, so that capitalist trade appears normal, like a 'regulative law of nature' (168), such as gravity. However, we can only comprehend social reality belatedly, or *post festum* (literally, 'after the party'). It is nearly impossible to perceive the emergence of new practices until after these have become familiar and seemingly the 'natural forms of social life' (168) or, as the saying goes, the way in which things have always been done. Once that has happened, we often do not try to analyse society as the result of the encounter between different social interests and classes, but turn instead to easier explanations like that of commodity fetishism, which presents the commodity as godlike and in control of human destiny.

Marx cautions us, though, against a new false pride in understanding the origin of the commodity fetish. Just because we understand how nature and society works, this does not mean that their effects spontaneously vanish. The 'scientific' discovery that air has certain chemical elements, like oxygen, has not changed the environment's physical configuration. Marx says that just because we understand aspects of capitalism, this does not mean that we have altered them; this underlines his rejection of idealist philosophy, the notion that the history of ideas changes social relations, rather than the reverse.

Recognizing the construction of social relations does, however, defamiliarize our commonsensical assumptions in ways that make them more open to critique as we turn

How to Read Marx's *Capital*

around to see what took place behind our backs. Marx *had* to start his analysis with the appearance of commodities to see the twofold nature of value, the twofold nature of labour, and their relation to money. He chose not to start with money and prices, as classical political economists often do, because the market place's rise and fall of prices 'conceals the social character of private labour and the social relations between the individual workers, by making those relations appear as relations between material objects, instead of revealing them plainly' (169). As a form, money cannot illustrate the divisions of labour because its currency hides these from plain sight.

Furthermore, unlike what bourgeois economists would have us believe, modern relations of market commodities are not eternal truths, but only hold true for certain kinds of societies, that is to say, capitalist ones. 'Political economists are fond of Robinson Crusoe stories' (169) that celebrate an individual's hard work as the key to success. Marx thinks that this is a stupid, if not intentionally confusing example, since Crusoe does not exist within a world of commodities, let alone capitalist exchanges. Crusoe's labour in making objects for his own use on the island does not produce commodities, since he lives in a world of personal use-value and does not produce to trade with anyone else. 'His stock-book contains a catalogue of the useful objects he possesses, of various operations necessary for their production, and finally of the labour-time that specific quantities of these products have on average cost him' (170). Crusoe's objects have no exchange-value, even though they have use-value for him: he does not need to express value through an abstraction like money, since he knows how much labour and time he requires to make one object rather than another. Because there is no social division of labour, there is no exchange-value. And without exchange-value, there is no profit. And without profit, as we shall see, there is no capitalism. Lastly, Crusoe does not fetishize his commodities, because he knows where their power came from: his own labour, which he has transferred, or objectified, into a useful object.

The fetishism of commodities also did not exist in pre-capitalist societies like medieval Europe. This form of society did not have independent individuals like Crusoe, since everyone was caught up in relations of collective subordination and domination, serfs to lords, laity to the Church. Unlike the modern market, which makes producers and consumers anonymous to each other, early modern hierarchies were known and visible to all. Since 'relations of personal dependence form the social foundation' in feudalism, as the serf annually owes labour directly to the manor's lord, there is 'no need for labour and its products to assume a fantastic form different from their reality'. Even though there is a division of labour in feudalism, 'whatever we might think' about the hierarchical

roles in which men confront each other in such a society, the social relations between individuals in the performance of their labour appear at all events as their own personal relations, and are not disguised as social relations between things, between the products of labour. (170)

What might a society without commodities look like? We would need to go back to 'the threshold of the history of all civilized peoples' to find 'the patriarchal rural industry of a peasant family which produces corn, cattle, yarn, linen and clothing for its own use' (171). While there might be division of labour, according to the family members' gender and age, these separations are not mediated through the exchange of commodities.

We could use this pastoral ideal to illustrate what a modern society that produces commodities, but without the supplement of commodity fetishism, might look like. This might be 'an association of free men, working with the means of production held in common, and expending their many different forms of labour-power in full self-awareness as one single social labour force' (171). Although Marx does not give a name to a society of interdependent labourers who might divide their tasks in transparent ways, but equally share in the ownership of the property, tools, and outcome of production, we can take this as his description of modern communism, rather than the earlier form of the idealized village mentioned above.

While the commodity-form 'makes its appearance at an early date' in Western history, it was not always the dominant form, since early modern trade relations often existed only in highly supervised pockets, usually limited to certain ethnic groups ('trading nations'), such as the Jews or Armenians, who were allowed to move between regions because they lacked their own nation-state. Today, however, we live in a world where it seems as if commodities belong to a nation of their own, a global market place complete with its own language. The globalized market is often presented in advertising as if its commodities have liberated themselves from the boringly local concerns of humans. As exchange-value becomes separated from use-value, it seems as if objects have needs of their own, which they satisfy by themselves in ways that divorce the representation of value from the 'social process' that created it.

Because the writers of 'political economy', the bourgeois defenders of the market, have 'incompletely' analysed labour as the source of value and labour-time as its measure, Marx argues that they have never asked about the historical origins of the current system, taking it to be an unquestioned advance over the past in the same way, Marx says, in which the Christian church sees pre-Christian religions as worthless. Within the mentality of bourgeois economists, modern society, with its division of labour, celebrates individual action outside of social constraints. This 'cult of abstract man' erases our collective relations, so that the idea of individuality becomes taken as the norm in a world that sees commodities as autonomous, outside of production, and only 'real' in the world of consumption (exchange). Marx later suggests that contemporary society fetishizes individuality in the same way as it fetishizes commodities; but, for now, just keep in mind how he relates economic practices to social formations.

Marx began this chapter by starting out with what seems obvious, the production of commodities, but through his discussion of the twofold nature of the commodity, he ends it by showing the 'secret' of the commodity: it appears to be powerful, but only because its human origins of value-production have been obscured. In the next chapter, Marx further pursues this argument as he turns to discuss the money-form.

Chapter 2. The Process of Exchange

This short chapter bridges the prior one on commodities and the following one on money as it reviews some themes that Marx has already introduced and propels them forward.

Marx reminds us that commodities cannot get up on their own legs, go to the market place, and exchange themselves. Only humans, 'the possessors of commodities', can do these things (178). In the market place, though, we approach others disguised as 'personifications of economic relations' (in the abstract roles of buyer and seller), rather than as actual humans embedded within economic relations, who exchange through the medium, or mediation, of a formal device like a contract.

While it might seem that trade simply involves the handing over of one commodity in exchange for another, in reality a new, intermediate, form of value emerges, the money-form, as a universal equivalent that allows for commodities to be exchanged. 'Money necessarily crystallizes out of the process of exchange' (181) because when commodities have exchanged hands, money remains ready to be used again for another trade.

As commodities are converted into an external standard, money, the products of labour undergo an 'alienation' (182) as they are now compared to something outside of themselves. In this sense, alienation means to cut something away from the whole, as a commodity's use-value is now divided and cast off from its exchange-value. In another sense, the word 'alienation' is also meant to suggest how commodities appear like 'alien' creatures once they are considered only in terms of their abstract exchange-value, rather than their use-value for humans.

Marx again repeats that this 'quantitative exchange-relation' historically first appears when different groups come to trade with one another at the borders between communities. In trade's early phases both the prices for goods and the first objects used for money seem to have been 'a matter of accident'. Initially, the items used as money were ones that came from outside the trading group, but were considered important (like cowry shells), or local items that had a high use-value and could be moved between people, 'for example cattle' (183). Because of their frequent contact with foreign groups, nomadic peoples were the first to develop the notion of money. Since highly mobile groups had to use something that was easily transportable, land was never considered to be exchangeable. Only with a highly developed bourgeois society, initially in the late 1600s and only on a large scale in the late eighteenth century during the French revolution, would property begin to be marketable. Before then, land was considered as fixed to noble lineages or ethnic communities; it was transferred only through marriage compacts, rather than commodity contracts.

As exchange becomes more prevalent, precious metals, like gold and silver, begin to be used as money because of their recognized uniform quality and ability to be 'divided at will' (184). Here Marx cautions against the notion that money is only a symbol, and could thus be replaced by other notations, like intangible credit. He mentions this not because the idea that a symbol can function as money is wrong (it is not, as we shall later see), but because at this point in his argument he wants to resist the notion that 'these characteristics are the arbitrary product of human reflection' (186), or that money, as well as all other human conventions, is simply a non-material matter of names, as Enlightenment philosophers tried to assert. The problem with moving too quickly to an argument about money as a symbolic form is that it ignores the historical process through which the modern form came about as well as money's linkage to the production of value in labour.

How to Read Marx's *Capital*

Furthermore, it leads to what Marx calls the 'money fetish', where 'relations of production therefore assume a material shape [as money] which is independent of their control and their conscious individual action' (187). A belief in 'the magic of money', as a commodity that can generate value by itself, is like the commodity fetish. How is it that money seems to contain value? This is the question Marx turns to in the next chapter.

Chapter 3. Money, or the Circulation of Commodities

Section 1. The Measure of Values

In the first section of this chapter, Marx defines money 'as a measure of value' which is 'the necessary form of appearance of the measure of value which is immanent in commodities, namely labour-time' (188). In this role, money standardizes different commodities in order to expand the domain of what can be traded. If we say that 20 yards of linen costs 12 pounds, and 1 coat costs 12 pounds, then 20 yards of linen ought to be traded for 1 coat. Here money does not actually carry any value within itself, all that it does is act as a convention to signify value in transit. Gold or silver, or any other material form of money, does have a use-value when it is used as a commodity to satisfy use needs, for example, as jewellery. But when these metals function as money, they are only 'imaginary or ideal' means of representing value and are considered to be use-less in the sense of only existing to act as a form for exchange-value.

Money expresses a commodity's value as its price. 'Price is the money-name of the labour objectified in a commodity' (195–6). Money, therefore, also functions as the 'standard for price' in addition to operating as a measure of value. A commodity's *price* (how much it costs, its quantitative number), is often confused with its *value* (the amount of labour-time it represents, its qualitative work), but these two functions are different. 'As measure of value, and as standard of price, money performs two quite different functions. It is the measure of value as the social incarnation of human labour; it is the standard of price as a quantity of metal with a fixed weight' (192). Historically, the names of money referred directly to this feature of weight, as 'the word pound . . . was the money-name given to an actual pound of silver' (194). This linkage changed as other substances, like copper or paper money, replaced the original metal alongside the 'continuous debasement of the currency by kings and princes', as they reduced the amount of the precious metal in each coin.

A commodity's price does not automatically reflect its value. Marx insists on distinguishing between a commodity's price in the market place and its actual value because the production of this difference is one of the defining features of capitalist practice. Not only is it possible for there to be a gap 'between price and magnitude of value' (196), but this separation is 'inherent in the price-form itself' (196); it is its purpose. The difference between price and value is absolutely vital to understand, since nearly all of Marx's ensuing arguments rest on understanding this.

Because value is the energy-transfer based on labour-time, Marx assumes that a commodity's value does not change. Value does not rise or fall through exchange, only the price of that value alters. One way to understand how an object might have a stable value, while having a fluctuating price, is to think of what happens when we go to a bank to borrow money. When we take out a loan, we are essentially buying money for immediate use, and the amount of interest we pay on the capital determines the price that the money will cost us. For the convenience of receiving the measure of value certified in money now, we pay a higher price for it: the original amount and the interest. If there's a fixed interest rate of 10 per cent, then we will pay the overall *price* of 11,000 pounds to buy the right to spend immediately the *value* of 10,000 pounds. I pay 11,000 to be given the equivalent of 10,000. If interest rates increase on the loan, the price of the borrowed money becomes higher and I might have to pay 12,000 for the value of 10,000. The underlying value of what I can purchase with this money remains the same. The only difference is that the price of the money has increased. The same process happens in reverse. When we deposit our money in a savings account, we are essentially selling our money to the bank, which pays us a higher price with the interest gained on our deposits.

Marx also illustrates how price can be entirely separated from value in certain instances. Some 'things' can be bought for a price even though they are value-less, in that they are not made by human labour, for instance 'conscience, honour, etc.' (197) We do not practise telling the truth in order to bring the value of our honesty to the market place, but we might sell it anyway for the right price. Indeed, since the price-form makes 'the exchangeability of commodities for money' (198) seem necessary, capitalism increasingly urges us to convert use-values into exchange-values and put a selling price on everything we hold dear.

Because the money-form is used as a form of appearance of both value and price, it works to paper over the difference between the two, since both are expressed in terms of money. Blurring the distinction, money increasingly seems to represent price alone, it 'ceases altogether to express value' (197). The move to talk about a commodity's price, rather than its value, is one more step towards mystifying the actual relations of production, since it is a further move to rely on abstract numbers, rather than material use. If money does not express value, it seems as if the market is simply a system for trading abstract prices, rather than values based on human production.

Notice that we have moved from a world of use-values to a world of exchange-values and then from a world of exchange-values to one of prices represented by money. Step by step, the practices of the market push us to move further away from the human source of value. Looking at a pile of coins, it is difficult to know from whence these coins came (from farm labour, from a factory, etc.). By entering a world of abstractions, our only guides seem to be money.

Section 2. The Means of Circulation

Having explained that money is a medium of value and standard of price, Marx now explains that money also acts as the means for circulating commodities. Remember that because money is the medium of exchange, the equation

commodity = use-value + exchange-value

becomes

commodity = use-value + money.

Yet we do not exchange use-values, since for Marx they are not exchangeable. 'Once a commodity has arrived at a situation in which it can serve as a use-value, it falls out of the sphere of exchange into that of consumption' (198). In this it appears as if the commodity's value is the exchanged money, since its use-value is ignored.

From this perspective, we have moved to a series of equivalents whereby a commodity can be exchanged for money, which, in turn, is exchanged for another commodity. Money acts as the means for transferring or circulating commodities in a process of exchange represented by the formula

commodity–money–commodity,

abbreviated as

C–M–C.

With trade that extends beyond the limits of a small enclosed group, commodities *must* be transformed into money, since money is the universal equivalent form. In this market relation, we also adopt a new social 'role'. Rather than entering the market as producers and consumers, we do so as interchangeable 'buyers' and 'sellers'. I go to the market with a commodity to look for a buyer who has money. I name my price, ideally the buyer agrees, and then gives me money in exchange for my commodity. She or he can then either consume the commodity (and realize its use-value) or turn around and sell it for more money. Similarly, I, who was formerly a seller, now take my money and try to buy something. In this concourse of buying and selling, a circuit of exchange (C–M–C) is created between a seller (who trades a commodity for money, C for M) and a buyer (who trades money for a commodity, M for C) through 'two metamorphoses of opposite yet mutually complementary character – the conversion of the commodity into money, and the re-conversion of the money into a commodity' (200).

Yet once someone has traded one commodity for another through the medium of money, money still remains after the exchange in the hand of whoever sold the commodity to the original buyers. Within capitalism, this money cannot really be allowed to sit still or be hoarded for fear of losing exchange-value. In the first stage, the seller of commodities seeks money. She or he assumes that because of competition, they will get a certain price. Yet while sellers assume that the price they will get for the commodity remains the same as it was in the past, they cannot be sure that when a product comes to the market it won't be 'superfluous, redundant and consequently useless' to the sellers. If I produce a commodity, like linen, and it has become cheaper in the interim because there are now too many weavers willing to sell the value of their labour-time through the form of their commodity for less money, then I will not get the same price as before. Because of the uncertainty of fluctuating prices, many sellers will seek to sell sooner rather than later so as to ensure that they get the price they had expected to get when making the commodity. Similarly, capitalists will see the leftover money as needing to be put back into circulation through the purchase of another commodity. Thus, the very presence of money speeds up the flow of exchanges.

This nervous need to increase the speed of exchanges constantly hovers in the mind of sellers, especially as it may foreshadow the onset of a larger economic crisis if there is a mismatch between the money that sellers want to receive and the money that buyers will give for certain commodities. Marx implies here that such a crisis is hard to resolve precisely because of the alienation that money creates. Since money, in the circulation of commodities, seems to be the real goal of exchange, it appears to have an even greater fetish-power than commodities, especially as money seems to have freed itself from determination by commodities. 'From the mere look of a piece of money, we cannot tell what breed of commodity has been transformed into it' (204). With ten British pounds in my pocket, you are ignorant of what has happened before this moment. 'Since every commodity disappears when it becomes money it is impossible to tell from the money itself how it got into the hands of its possessor, or what article has been changed into it' (205). Money's abstract numbers do not say anything about the kind of labour that went into making the commodity or even what kind of commodity was sold to make money.

Money's abstraction and need for speed pushes traders to expand commerce beyond familiar boundaries and become incorporated within a wider and more complex social space. Since the circulation of commodities is no longer a 'direct exchange of products', but an exchange that goes through a mobile medium, money allows for a geographic expansion of the realm of trade beyond what was possible in barter, when both traders had to bring their goods to a meeting place. As more and more commodities can be equated to each other through money, the chain of commodity exchanges grows, bringing us into a 'whole network of social connections . . . entirely beyond the control of the human agents' (207). Like it or not, we are caught within a mesh of trade far beyond the local regions of regionalized trade where there was a direct exchange of commodities or, at least, a very basic use of money-form. A new sense of unfamiliar space, the global market, emerges, along with our interdependence with other participants in the market whom we might never see or even know about their existence.

> Circulation bursts through all the temporal, spatial and personal barriers imposed by the direct exchange of products, and it does this by splitting up the direct identity present in this case between the exchange of one's own product and the acquisition of someone else's into the two antithetical segments of sale and purchase. (209)

Yet as money makes it easier to connect to faraway markets, it also amplifies the possibility of an economic crisis. For in this expanded realm, there is no guarantee that the two ends of a commodity chain, a buyer and seller, will always connect, often leaving money left over that is not delivering any use-value or exchange-value. Even in the normal state of affairs, 'circulation sweats money from every pore' (208) after commodities have been bought and sold. Whichever capitalist has this money, she or he will want to use it to buy more commodities, and begin the 'constant and monotonous repetition of the same process' of commodity circulation all over again (210–11). The larger effect here is that because money emerges from the circuit of C–M–C exchange, it seems as if money, rather than commodities, is the point of exchange.

This belief in the primacy of money leads to false conclusions about its power to determine price. While the price of a commodity tends to settle into an expected range, sometimes the price rises, what we call inflation, or falls, what we call deflation. Marx disagrees with liberal economists who believe that inflation is caused by an oversupply of circulating money; Marx instead insists that inflation is caused by the oversupply of value-producing labour. After gold and silver were discovered in the New World during the seventeenth and eighteenth centuries, there was a steady fall in what gold and silver coins could buy, that is to say, the prices for commodities rose. Marx says the claim that the proliferation of precious metals led to inflation was a 'false conclusion' (214). Though Marx does not explicitly say why, his implied answer might be that the period's inflation came about due to the discovery of New World mines, which were largely excavated using cheap native or imported African slave labour, rather than European wage-labourers. The value of the gold and silver currency decreased, since it was suddenly easier to find gold and silver and less valuable labour was used to mine the metals. Prices may rise and fall, but they do so solely in relationship to labour costs, not to the relative amount of money, which is just the symbolic notation for the value that labour creates.

On the other hand, while the mass of money does not matter, the velocity of its circulation (or what is today called liquidity) does. For if money 'slows down or completely leaves the sphere of circulation', this slows down the cycle of exchanges. Like a shark that dies if motionless, capitalism requires the 'hurried nature of society's metabolic process, the quick disappearance of commodities from the sphere of circulation, and their equally quick replacement by fresh commodities' (217). The importance of speed means that ultimately there is no reason why we need to have gold as money (as coins). Money could as easily be paper notes, which are faster and easier to transport, thus facilitating exchange. If money can be dematerialized from metal to paper, there is also no reason why it cannot be further dematerialized to go from being actual paper notes to computer-screen notations of credit, which is even easier to move around distant buyers and sellers. Consider how frequently our current transactions are electronic, as we further and further abstract our exchanges. The need for speed leads Marx to the next section, on money itself.

Section 3. Money

Money is the commodity that is both a measure of value and a medium of circulation (227). Because it has these functions, people often hoard money in the belief that they are protecting their value from the vagaries of the market's turbulence. In this section, Marx argues against the mercantilist notions that holding gold reserves ensures a nation's wealth by storing value. Marx wants to show why hoarding coins ('the greed for gold') is contradictory and self-defeating for capitalists. The miser who holds on to her or his money makes the mistake of thinking that the coins contain value. But coins do not have value; they are simply a denominating measure of value, which is a social form, not a private one. Hoarders think that exchange-values are really use-values and that money has value, especially outside of the mobile exchange, when in reality it is only the medium that helps catalyse exchange. If I save Deutschmarks in the 1980s because I believe they have intrinsic value, then in ten years, I will be shocked to discover that they are worthless, since the money-form has been changed to Euros.

In societies that are not dominated by capitalist procedures, such as nomadic groups or feudal peasants, hoarding does have some effect because these peoples have a 'traditional mode of production, aimed at fulfilling their own requirements' corresponding 'to a fixed and limited range of needs' (228) that ensures prices remain stable, even if only by recourse to the moral pressure of not changing what has become customary. With groups that have not largely entered into the outward-expanding network of commodity circulation, money can functionally remain simply a measure of value. But 'with more developed commodity production', it is less possible to remove money from circulation, since these societies see currency transfers as a source of wealth-making. In this world-view, money is desirable when it is put into motion to create accumulation, not when it rests in a hoard.

In times of crisis, though, the middle class, which has risen through the circulation of values, 'declares money to be a vain imagination. Commodities alone are money' (236). During financial emergencies (like stock market downturns), people rush to buy something tangible, like houses. What these investors forget is that the house is also an object of exchange and can lose its price as easily as can stocks or bonds. For Marx, the belief that objects are more real than currency is nonsensical, because commodities also only have value as they are part of the circulation of money. The only relatively stable method for retaining value is through use-value, where commodities are used, rather than seen as a form for exchange. Capitalists, however, have got themselves too far in the mud to go back to a world of use-values. Keep in mind the underlying logic of inexorable development here. Once we seem to step onto the path leading to a commodity society, there is no safe way of turning back. Crisis looms.

The other problem with hoarding is that by slowing the circulation of money it aggravates tensions between creditor and debtors. As hoarders refuse to release money, they make it harder for their debtors to get hold of the money necessary for loan repayments. A monetary crisis erupts when the 'ongoing chain of payments' has been disturbed in this way. Historically, this crisis led to the development of intangible credit money, which seeks to reduce the possible number of obstacles in trading purely for money. But even fictional credit can still disappear in times of panic.

Finally, money acts as world money by allowing traders to break out of their local regional barriers and insert themselves within interconnected segments of the world market's commodity chains. 'It is in the world market that money first functions to its full extent as the commodity whose natural form is also the directly social form of realization of human labour in the abstract' (241). Hence 'countries with developed bourgeois production limit the hoards concentrated in the strong rooms of the banks to a minimum required for the performance of their specific functions' lest the build-up of these hoards creates blockages in the global circulation of commodities. Marx suggests that more developed nations will force less integrated ones into the world market as a means of rebalancing the capitalist system. By accelerating time expectations for repayment and injecting the need to accumulate by investment, dominant nations prevent weaker ones from holding on to their goods or natural resources because they need to get money back to pay their loans.

Part Two: The Transformation of Money into Capital

Chapter 4. The General Formula for Capital

In the last part, Marx argued backwards from the presence of a terrific production of commodities to show that the exchange of commodities increasingly requires the presence of money as a measure of value, standard of price, means of circulation, store of value, and means of payment, especially as world money. Again, we need to emphasize that Marx does not consider the presence of money as a defining feature of capitalism. Capitalism requires the emergence of the money-form, but money is also necessary as a means of calibrating the trade of two different kinds of commodities in all societies that have complex divisions of labour and engage in long-distance trade. Marx's interest is in how money becomes used as a building block for the rise of capital. Notice that the first part was called 'Commodities and Money' and described the transformation of commodities into money. This part is called 'The Transformation of Money into Capital'. *Capital*, not *Money*, is the title of Marx's book.

By this chapter's end, Marx will have differentiated money from capital, which he defines as money that is invested to make more money. He declares that capitalism's fundamental logic, what he calls the General Formula for Capital, is the use of money to buy a commodity only in order to sell it for profit. Money traded for more money through the medium of a commodity is 'transformed into capital' (248).

If we look at the circulation of commodities as a form of exchanging use-values, we can witness the onset of the 'economic form brought into being by this process', 'find that its ultimate product is money', and see that money 'is the first form of appearance of capital', the first expression of exchange-value (247). Marx says that 'the circulation of commodities is the starting-point of capital' and the development of 'the production of commodities and their circulation in its developed form, namely trade' forms the historic preconditions 'under which capital arises. World trade and the world market date from the sixteenth century, and from then on the modern history of capital starts to unfold' (247). Though Marx does not specifically mention what happened in the sixteenth century that began the world market (or, at least Europeans' entry into pre-existing Middle and Far Eastern trading circuits), it helps to consider the warlike explorations into the New World by Europeans as helping to inaugurate their world trade, as the natural and mineral resources of the New World gave Europeans access to commodities that they could exchange in African, Middle Eastern, and Asian markets.

Historically, 'capital first confronts landed property [such as that of the nobility or the Church] in the form of money' with 'merchants' capital and usurers' capital' (247). The early capitalist interests used trading and lending capital, rather than money invested in land, because religious and

How to Read Marx's *Capital*

noble groups 'hoard' the resources of land, thus making it difficult to commoditize.

The first distinction between 'money as money and money as capital' involves their respective sequences. We saw that the circulation of commodities uses money as money, a medium to trade commodities: C–M–C, 'selling in order to buy'. But alongside this there is another process that inverts the order to become M–C–M, where one starts with money as capital, buying a commodity to sell it. The C–M–C sequence of trading one commodity for another through the medium of money ultimately still remains based on use-values. The inverted order of M–C–M, wherein money is the beginning and end of a series, is based on exchange-value.

With M–C–M, if a buyer bought 100 pounds' worth of goods, it would be 'absurd' for her or him then to sell these commodities to end up with 100 pounds. That would just be exchanging money for money, and only a foolish person would go to the effort of trading for exchange-value and not make a profit. If all that the buyer was going to do was end up with the same amount of money, she or he might just as well have saved the effort and simply hoarded it. If I send money out to get money back in, this reflux needs to bring back more money than it began with.

Therefore, Marx says the circuit, money for commodity for money, means that the capitalist in the end must have more money, the original sum (M) plus a profit (Δ). Δ (pronounced 'delta') is scientific notation for change.

This formula is

$$M–C–(M + \Delta M).$$

Alternatively, M + ΔM can be represented as M' (pronounced 'M-prime'), so the formula reads M–C–M', where M' = M + ΔM.

The money created through the circuit of exchange is the 'increment or excess over the original value'. Marx calls this excess 'surplus-value', (251) as the value that is not from use-value and is greater than the original amount of exchange-value. If circulated exchange-value creates surplus-value, then Marx says that it has been 'valorized', meaning that value has been added; it is valorization that 'converts [money] into capital'.

Here we have Marx's definition of capital. Capital is money that is invested to create profit. Capital is not money used to satisfy a use-value, but money that is spent only to create surplus-value. Because surplus-value only emerges through exchange, the circulation of commodities, the capitalist's goal is never to end with a commodity that could be consumed for its use-value, and not even for 'profit on any single transaction. His aim is rather the unceasing movement of profit-making' (254). Since exchange-value exists outside of human needs, because it is alienated from human requirements, capital consequently imagines a world in which accumulation is 'an end in itself, for the valorization of value takes place only within this constantly renewed movement. The movement of capital is therefore limitless' (253).

This restless, never-ending process of accumulation differentiates a miser hoarding money from a capitalist. The miser holds on to money because he believes that he can secure its imagined exchange-value, and, perversely, turns the desire for money into a use-value: the pleasure of hoarding. Capitalists, on the other hand, are only concerned for the market place's circuit of exchange; they must throw money 'again and again into circulation' (255), since each new cycle of trade sweats out money as it ends, ideally with more surplus-value being created. Now we can understand why Marx emphasizes the velocity of circulation, since profit is achieved only when the circuit of exchange has been completed. The capitalist always desires to reduce the time that it takes to complete a trade cycle, since the faster the circuit turns, the more profit is made. Time delays mean inactive, hence lost, capital.

In the simple form of circulation, there was a fetishism of commodities, as it seemed that commodities gained a 'form independent of their use-values' and their human producers. But in a world run by the principle of M–C–M', it seems as if commodities are the medium between money, rather than the reverse, and can thus be squeezed out of the formula. This move makes it appear as if money has a relationship only with itself and it creates a money-fetish in which it seems as if 'money begets money', without the need for the intermediate social stage of the commodity-form or the humans that create these commodities. By looking to circulation of currency as the source of profit, the capitalist then creates a market-fetish, which treats the sphere of exchange as a living thing. Think, for instance, how frequently people will talk about making money from the stock market, as if value comes from buying and selling, rather than making and using. Marx turns to critique this notion in the next chapter, but ends this one by saying that the General Formula for Capital is M–C–M' – money used to create profit.

Chapter 5. Contradictions in the General Formula

After having shown that surplus-value is created at the end of a cycle, Marx then says that this does not make any sense. Where does the surplus-value (profit) come from? For despite what capitalists say, we know that inanimate money cannot make more money, just as commodities cannot bring themselves to the market. There has to be a source of profit that we are missing.

To get at this problem of the missing value, Marx reaffirms that commodities cannot be sold for more or less than their value, since value comes from labour-time expended in producing the commodity, and the amount invested into an object cannot be changed, gained, or lost within the market place's circulation. 'Circulation, or the exchange of commodities, creates no value' (266). Furthermore, if I choose to sell a commodity for less than its value, and do not make up for this loss in some other way, then, over the long run, I will go bankrupt. In the market place, I can, however, realize a gap between a commodity's value and its price. A commodity can be bought or sold for a price that does not reflect the commodity's real value and this difference is the gained surplus-value (now we can begin to see why the value/price distinction is important).

Liberal economists claim that buyers and sellers exchange goods to satisfy each other's use needs, but this is contradicted by the end result, as only one of them ultimately profits. Marx admits that in one sense the liberal political economists are right: 'in so far as use-values are concerned, it is clear that both parties may gain' (259). Because use-value is a qualitative need, each side can feel that what they required has been achieved. It is 'otherwise with exchange-value'. Since exchange-value is a quantitative matter, it is not mathematically possible for one side to gain surplus if both receive equal amounts of exchange-value through trade.

One possible solution to this paradox might be if one side profits because the seller trades her or his commodity for more or less than its actual value. This is not a real solution given that a seller of commodities receives money to buy new commodities. If I sell my goods for less money, allowing the buyer to make a profit, then when I turn around to buy new ones, I'll have less money and will need, in turn, to buy goods for less then their value. What the person who sells to me gains in the first round of exchange, she or he will lose in the next. In this way, losses and gains even out and no surplus-value is created. We still have not solved the puzzle of profit.

Where else might surplus-value come from? It might come from a buyer cheating a seller by forcing them to sell a commodity for a price less than its value. But Marx claims: 'the capitalist class of a given country, taken as a whole, cannot defraud itself' (266). While cheating may go on, capitalists cannot, as a general rule, consistently rely on profit from defrauding each other, since every capitalist, as mentioned above, is at various times both a seller and buyer. Whatever advantage capitalists might gain as sellers by cheating, they would lose as buyers at the next moment, when they in turn are cheated. Because of the twofold nature of the capitalist, as buyer and seller, profit cannot systematically come from mutual cheating (although Marx realizes that capitalists have the benefits of nationalism and can cheat weaker foreign capitalists knowing that they cannot retaliate).

Some believe that profit emerges from rising prices due to inflation. This cannot explain the problem for two reasons. Firstly, inflation affects both buyers and sellers equally, and it does not change the ratios of money involved. Secondly, as Marx explained, a commodity's price is not the same thing as its value. Simply because the price of a good has gone up, it does not mean that its value has done so. The price rise is a fictional bubble ready to burst.

There are two groups who do seem to make money through exchange: long-distance merchants, who buy goods cheaply in one port and transport them to another to sell them more expensively, and usurers, who charge interest on loans. 'Buying in order to sell dearer, is at its purest in genuine merchants' capital' (266). But because 'the whole of this movement takes place within the sphere of circulation' (that is to say neither involved with production or consumption, but simply distribution) the merchant has to be thought of as just an intermediary 'who parasitically inserts himself' between 'selling and buying producers' to cheat both of them. Because the merchant depends on others to initiate and complete exchanges, mercantile capital could never become the dominant form of profit-making, especially as it is highly vulnerable to global changes that it cannot control.

The same is true for usurers, those who make profit from lending money. Ultimately, 'merchants' capital and interest-bearing capital are derivative forms' that rely on other traders, and they cannot be used to explain the contradiction of surplus created through circulation. On the other hand, Marx says, 'it will become clear why, historically, these two forms appear before the modern primary form of capital' (267). This does not seem very clear. Marx seems to be contradicting himself by saying that merchants' and usurers' capital both seems to help start modern capitalism and yet cannot explain its operation. By the last part of the volume, he will return to explaining this riddle, but for now we must momentarily accept his claim about the lack of importance of mercantile and money-lending capitalism.

So if profit does not come from the relations between capitalists buying and selling from one another, where does the surplus come from? The main contradiction of the General Formula for Capital is that profit comes from circulation and yet, seemingly, cannot come from circulation. 'Capital cannot therefore arise from circulation', since that profit cannot come from buyers and sellers cheating each other. 'It is equally impossible for [capital] to arise apart from circulation', since circulation is where exchange-value is realized in ways that create surplus-value. Marx recognizes that it does not make sense that capital 'must have its origin both in circulation and not in circulation' (268–9). If the General Formula for Capital is that capital is money invested to make profit, the contradiction in this formula is that we still do not know *how* profit is really made. How can we resolve this paradox? The answer lies in the next chapter.

Chapter 6. The Sale and Purchase of Labour-Power

The riddle of surplus-value's origin cannot also be determined in 'money itself, since in its functions as a means of purchase and payment it does no more than realize the price of the commodity it buys or pays for' (270). Money is just a medium that brings together different commodities, but it is not a use-value or actual source of value. The possessor of money must instead look for a 'special commodity' that can create value. Remember that for Marx, all value is created from labour. Since capitalists do not labour, they cannot create value. Who creates value then? Those that do labour: the labouring class. Since only labour creates value, the surplus-value creating commodity must be 'the capacity for labour, in other words labour-power' (270). For money to be transformed into capital, for money to create surplus-value (profit), it must buy a value-producing commodity. This commodity is labour-power.

Marx defines labour-power as 'the aggregate of those mental and physical capacities existing in the physical form, the living personality, of a human being, capabilities which he sets in motion whenever he produces a use-value of any kind' (270). He then conditions this definition by saying that labour-power can 'appear on the market as a commodity only if . . . the possessor, the individual whose labour-power it is, offers it for sale or sells it as a commodity'. There is a key difference between labour, which makes value, and labour-power, which is a fraction of human labour sold as a commodity. Labour-power is commodified labour that is mainly bought by capitalists to create surplus-value.

For the labourer to sell his labour-power within the market place, two historical conditions have to be met. Firstly, the labourer must 'be the free proprietor of his own labour-capacity, hence his person'. Workers must be able to alienate their labour by selling a part of it for a price. In order for the labourers to be able to commodify their vitality, they cannot be either slaves or serfs. When a slave is sold, the purchaser buys the slave's entire body including all of its labour and rest, not just a fraction of it. Serfs bound to the land, likewise, must give their lord a set amount of their labour annually as part of the customary agreement, but this labour is not sold. The agreements are either arranged by long custom or by political settlement after invasion, but not by the price-setting market place. Labourers must be 'free' from pre-modern masters and lords who dictate their movement.

The 'second essential condition which allows the owner of money to find labour-power in the market as a commodity' is that the seller of labour-power, the worker, must have 'no other commodity for sale' than his labour (272). The labourer must be 'free' of any 'means of production, such as raw materials, instruments of labour, etc.' that they could use to survive outside of the labour market. Just why the worker does not have anything else to sell does not interest 'the owner of money' and, for the moment, it is not Marx's concern either (he will come to this later, in Part Eight). The definition of a proletarian is someone who has only their labour to sell. While we often think of a proletarian as a factory labourer, Marx uses the term more broadly, in ways that arguably encompass most kinds of labour today.

Marx emphasizes that the creation of a 'free' person is a historically new feature, something that defines modernity. The emergence of an individual subject who 'alienates' their labour by commodifying it because they have nothing else to sell 'has no basis in natural history, nor does it have a social basis common to all periods of human history' (273). This scenario occurs *only* in a capitalist mode of production after a series of 'many economic revolutions' involving prior complex divisions of labour that can be gauged by the ways in which the form of money's use has been changed through different phases as 'the mere equivalent of commodities', a 'means of circulation', a 'means of payment', a 'hoard', and 'world currency'.

Neither the 'feeble circulation of commodities', nor the 'mere circulation of money' can be used to define the start of a capitalist era. These are only symptoms of a larger shift in the mode of production. Capital, as a 'new epoch in the process of social production', begins 'only when the owner of the means of production and subsistence finds the free worker available, on the market, as the seller of his own labour-power' (274). Capitalism is a distinctly new historical phase because the conditions of unfree, bound labour, different from slavery or vassalage, could not have dominantly existed in pre-modern (here pre-1500s) Western society.

If labour-power is a commodity, how do we determine its value? Its value comes from the duration of labour-time necessary to generate 'the means of subsistence necessary for the maintenance of its owner' (274) or what Marx calls necessary labour. A worker sells a unit of his labour-time for money (wages) to purchase what he needs in order to satisfy his survival needs, no matter how widely we define these basic needs. While Marx lists basic needs as mainly involving food, clothing, fuel, housing, and education/training, he admits that these needs are relative and depend on the climate and environment of the worker and the historical conditions of her or his society. A Westerner's 'habits and expectations' make him consider his basic needs as being different from, and probably more than, those of someone in a non-Western society. Just as Marx does not question the morality of use needs, so, too, does he forgo judgement on what workers consider to be their basic needs.

Marx also significantly considers subsistence needs as not only covering those of the individual worker, but also the needs of the worker's entire family, including his partner

How to Read Marx's *Capital*

and children (or other future replacements) as the expanded set of the individuals who feed and nurture the worker, so that he can return to labour, and those for whom the labourer works to provide. The value of labour-power is thus determined not only by the value necessary for the individual's self-regeneration, but also by the costs of social reproduction, the support of the next generation. Notice an unsaid shift here. In earlier chapters, Marx argued that value can be determined by the amount of abstract labour-time, a social average of labour skills. Now Marx begins the process of providing a more concrete and material understanding of a previously conceptual term when he now defines the value of labour not as labour-time in the abstract, but as labour-time for human survival and welfare.

Once we recognize that the only commodity that a capitalist can purchase to create value is human labour-power, we have moved closer to understanding how surplus-value can be generated. Surplus-value is not made by generally trading commodities in the market place, but with the sale of a unique commodity, labour-power. The only commodity that has value is workers' labour-power, since value is only created by labour. However, workers do not get the true price for the value of their labour. Surplus-value emerges from the difference between the price (wage) given to the worker for the value of her or his labour-power.

Marx then was not completely forthcoming when he earlier said that there is not any cheating within a capitalist economy. For while one nation's capitalists might not systematically cheat the other capitalists of that land, they do systematically cheat the members of another non-capitalist class: labourers. This fraud is the origin and sole source of surplus-value.

To be clear, according to Marx, neither exchange nor the use of money makes a society capitalist. Capitalism is specifically the social system that restlessly seeks profit, and it gains this profit from exploiting labourers. In a society based on exchange-values, it would be silly for capitalists to give up the surplus-values they gain. Yet for a society that bases itself on use-values, and is thus uninterested in making profits, such a reduction makes sense. The former is capitalism, the latter socialism. If labourers were paid the true value of their work, there would be no price differentials, no surplus-value, no profits, and no capital. Against this, the demand for 'social justice' fundamentally means that all parts of society should be compensated for the real value of their work.

We might ask, why do workers put up with constantly being cheated by capitalists? Marx's answer is historical. While labourers before the onset of capitalism needed certain commodities to survive (like food, housing, etc.), they also partially controlled their own means of production. In pre-modern society, serfs may have been *oppressed* by the nobility, as they were coerced to work for the manor, but they were not *exploited* in having to sell their labour-power. Furthermore, serfs often had small farms of their own as well as customary rights to use communally shared land, both of which gave them a small resource on which to survive.

In the move to modernity, with the advent of capitalist agriculture, serfs are 'freed' from their historical obligations to remain on land. This is a false freedom, since the serf usually becomes liberated from the land by being forced off it and prevented from using the commons. Because de-ruralized labourers must buy things to live which they could

How to Read Marx's *Capital*

previously have either made for themselves or traded in barter-like exchanges, they have to go to the market place with only one thing to sell, themselves, i.e. their labour-power. This is especially true if the serf or worker does not own any tools, while the capitalist does (for instance, a factory worker can only make things by being 'allowed' to use the factory).

Because the labourer needs money now and cannot refuse work and wait for better wages in the face of hunger and other survival needs, she or he is in a position of weakness when bargaining for wages. Therefore, workers are structurally disempowered and vulnerable to having to sell the value of their work for a low price. Furthermore, the buyer of labour-power, the boss, is able to hold on to the labourer's wages until the labourer has made the commodities that will be sold.

To press this point about unfairness further, Marx sees the language of freedom and equality in the market place as a mystifying deception. The capitalist says that in the sphere of the market place, there are only individual buyers and sellers, not social classes or group interests. For the capitalists who structurally benefit from the sphere of circulation, the market place of commodity exchange presents itself as 'a very Eden of the innate rights of man' of 'Freedom, Equality, Property and Bentham'. Everyone is equally free to buy and sell (labour-power) as they wish: individualistic 'free will' and universal rights for all in the exchange between the worker and the employer. They have 'property rights' over what they wish to sell and can look to their own advantage and the satisfaction of their needs (this is what Marx is alluding to when he includes the name of the utilitarian philosopher [Jeremy] Bentham in his list).

The image of the market as a utopian space of freedom and equality, however, covers up the pre-existing inequalities between worker and boss. There is a saying, attributed to Anatole France, that wryly illustrates Marx's point about the free choice to sell one's labour or not. The saying is that the rich and poor are equally free to sleep under the bridge at night. The grim joke here is that only the rich have the choice not to sleep under the bridge. Those who are too poor to afford housing do not. A similar result of unequal power appears after the one who buys labour-power with money and its seller are finished exchanging. Now

> the money-owner . . . strides out in front as a capitalist; the possessor of labour-power follows as his worker. The one smirks self-importantly and is intent on business; the other is timid and holds back, like someone who has brought his own hide to market and now has nothing else to expect but – a tanning. (280)

Once we recognize labour-power as the unique source of surplus-value, we have solved the riddle of the General Formula for Capital's contradiction. If capital is money invested to make profit, then this profit does not come from one capitalist cheating another, but from one capitalist cheating those who have nothing to sell but their own labour as a commodity. We can also now understand why commodities and money might be fetishized as creating value. Because the price the worker has been paid to make the object is less than the value of human energy transferred from the worker to the object, it seems as if the created surplus-value was made by the commodity itself, since, in the sphere of exchange we cannot see what has been behind our backs, the exploitation of the worker in the sphere of production. In reality, commodities and money are only the 'forms of appearance' through which the labourer's value is carried. In appearance, it seems as if commodities and money are actually the source of value. Yet once we understand the real origin of surplus-value, we can demystify the commodity's effects. Think back to *Capital*'s first line about capitalist society's monstrous increase in the production of commodities. Now that we know that commodities are produced within a capitalist society for the sale of profit that emerges from the exploitation of labourers, we might rephrase this line to define capitalism as the kind of society that vastly increases the exploitation of producers.

In the first two parts, Marx started with the commodity to show how it becomes money, and then depicted how money becomes capital. In this process, we have understood how the difference between the price of labour-power and its value creates surplus-value. Yet to completely perceive the ways in which this gap is made, we need to leave the 'sphere of circulation', the market place, which only trades, but does not create value, and enter the 'hidden abode of production' (279), where value is actually made through the transfer of human labour into commodities. The 'secret of profit-making' can only be laid bare by unveiling this place that is otherwise closed off from public inspection.

Part Three: The Production of Absolute Surplus-Value

Marx changes his viewpoint in the next two parts of *Capital*. The first two, more theoretical, parts investigated the nature of value. Marx has looked at the realm of circulation to explore why the commodity seems to be the unit of capital, as a profit-bearing object, but he has not yet explained how surplus profit is actually taken from labour-power. In other words, he has an explanation for the exploitation of labourers, but now needs to illustrate its practice in the realm of production. For readers of *Capital*, this means that Marx spends less time deciphering capitalism's abstractions and more on its material practices. The next two parts are essentially Marx's history of the stages of Western capitalism's development. These sections are the ones that give *Capital* its ethical edge as they describe in detail the miserable living and working conditions that the labouring classes endure.

Chapter 7. The Labour Process and the Valorization Process

Section 1. The Labour Process

Marx started the first part by defining what he meant by a commodity (something which is made to be exchanged with others in order for the producer to receive something that is useful) and what made a commodity a capitalist commodity (when commodities are only made to be sold for surplus-value [profit], which is created by unpaid labour).

In this section, Marx now turns to the relation between labour and surplus-value. He begins by describing the non-capitalist features of labour so that he can, in turn, describe the specific features of labour conditions within capitalism. For Marx, labour is the 'process between man and nature . . . by which man, through his own actions, mediates, regulates and controls the metabolism between himself and nature' (283). The difference between human and animal interaction with nature is that human activity is premeditated.

> A spider conducts operations which resemble those of a weaver, and a bee would put many a human architect to shame by the construction of its honeycomb cells. But what distinguishes the worst architect from the best of bees is that the architect builds the cell in his mind before he constructs it in wax. (284)

'Apart from the exertion' of the body, a 'purposeful will is required'. This component of human thought and creativity is vital, since the more repetitive, mechanical, and mindless the work, the more degrading it becomes. This theme of dehumanizing work continues throughout Marx's account as a feature of capitalism's destructive nature.

Marx now categorizes the three elements of the labour process as work (human purposeful activity); the object of the work (nature); and instruments (tools) used by humans on nature. Marx immediately drops out of consideration anything that nature 'freely' provides, but he does include as 'raw materials' natural resources that have been 'filtered through previous labour', like felled trees, which have 'already undergone some alteration by means of labour' (284–5). The instruments of labour vary according to human development, and phases of human history are often commonly defined by the kinds of tools that were produced in these periods (for instance, the 'iron age' the 'stone age'). Marx, however, defines historical stages according to the *mode of production*, as the relationships of labour's organization and process of value creation, rather than the *means of production*, which he defines as including only the tools and nature (287). While the transformation of tools can provide an index to social changes, neither tools nor the environmental objects of labour create value. The historical change in the kinds of instruments used during any period ought instead to be read as a symptom, or form of appearance, that indicates a transformation in the organization of society and its work process.

The good sense of Marx's distinction comes when we consider that new inventions are often not widely implemented until the social conditions for their use makes them viable. One example might be the internet, which existed decades before its popularization in the late 1980s and early 1990s in the industrialized nations as commercial needs for information flow invigorated its use. The internet became a mainstream tool only when information-driven financial schemes began to become a dominant aspect of Western economies.

A machine which is not active in the labour process is useless. In addition, it falls prey to the destructive power of natural processes. Iron rusts; wood rots. Yarn with which we neither weave nor knit is cotton wasted. Living labour must seize on these things, awaken them from the dead, change them from merely possible into real and effective use-values. (289)

Tools by themselves do nothing.

The labour process within capitalism has two more defining features. Firstly, 'the worker works under the control of the capitalist', who has bought labour-power and can control the labourer's work (291). While the labourer is dubiously 'free' to commodify her or his labour and sell it on the market place, once having done so, she or he must submit to the buyer of that labour as a boss. In this way, labourers become more like bees: they no longer premeditate their labour, which is controlled by the capitalist's prerogative. Secondly, the resulting 'product is the property of the capitalist and not that of the worker, its immediate producer' (292). Workers are separated from the possession of what they make, and have little to show for their work when it is all done, other than money in the form of wages, which must be spent soon to restore their energy and provide shelter, etc.

Section 2: The Valorization Process

When labourers work, they produce use- and exchange-values. The capitalist, however, is only interested in the valorization of exchange-value. The capitalist has not spent money to make use-values, he wants to create surplus exchange-value, which must come through the medium of a use-value. The capitalist's 'aim is to produce not only a use-value, but a commodity; not only use-value, but [exchange-]value; and not just [exchange-]value, but also surplus-value' (293). The work process must valorize the produced commodities in ways that deliver profit.

The capitalist spends money to buy commodities that will be used to make a coat: cotton, equipment, labour-power. These human and non-human commodities do not deliver surplus-value, since the materials and the instruments used to make the end product only transfer their value to the final product. Having spent money on commodities that can make a coat, the capitalist could sell it for the price that reflects the combined value of the commodities used to make it. Doing so, though, the capitalist 'stares in astonishment. The value of the product is equal to the value of capital advanced. The value advanced has not been valorized, no surplus-value has been created, and consequently money has not been transformed into capital' (297–8). Now the capitalist grows angry. Why did he expend all this time and effort to make something that was not profitable? Does not he deserve something for his time?

If materials and the instruments of production do not add value, then it must come from the other purchased element: the worker's labour-power. Marx now significantly notes that the amount of labour-time that a worker needs to create the value to trade for his basic needs (what Marx later calls necessary labour) is less than the value he might actually provide in the end to the capitalist. Even though the 'daily sustenance of labour-power costs only half a day's labour', the worker often hands over the 'value of a day's labour-power' (301). If the worker had sold a half-day's labour, there would have been a fair and equal exchange. But when the labourer works a whole day for a price that only reflects the value he needs to survive, then he has unwittingly sold her or his labour-time for *less than its value*. There is a gap between what *price* the employer has paid for labour-time in the form of wages and the *value* created by that labour. The difference between the price paid for labour-time and its value is the extra or surplus-value that the worker has effectively 'given' to the employer for free. The riddle of surplus-value is thus solved.

When the capitalist sells a good in the market place, he sells it for *all the value* that the worker has put into it, but he has only paid the worker for the value that the labourer needs to exist. The profit that emerges from the circulation of commodities does not come from the commodity itself, money, or even market-place exchange, but from *unpaid labour*. Since labour is the sole source of value, unpaid labour is the source of all surplus-value. Had the worker been paid for the full value of her or his labour, no surplus-value would have been created. Thus, the capitalist's main interest is to create a social environment and work processes that allow him to appropriate unremunerated labour from his workers (that is to say, to exploit them).

Before considering how capitalism gets this unpaid labour, Marx emphasizes that skilled labour does not necessarily create more value than unskilled labour, because the cost of skilled labour must take the value of the skilled labourer's training into account. Remember that Marx said that education (or workplace training) was as much a basic human need as food, clothing, and shelter. Once the investment of time for teaching, studying, and examining for a professional's training has been removed from the equation, her or his labour should essentially be no more valuable than that of an industrial worker. Having clarified this point, Marx turns to consider the parts that go into making capital.

Chapter 8. Constant Capital and Variable Capital

The twofold nature of labour involves the difference between labour that is needed to earn the things that preserve a labourer's life and labour that is in excess of these needs. This distinction parallels the now familiar twofold nature of the commodity (use- and exchange-value). The labourer creates the value that she or he will 'use', while then continuing to create surplus-value that will be 'carried' with the commodity to be realized in the market place. In this chapter, Marx returns to his definition of labour (labour, objects, and tools) to make another twofold distinction between *constant capital* and *variable capital*, which can also be understood as capital for use and capital for exchange.

Constant capital is 'that part of capital . . . which is turned into means of production' (raw material, additional material, and instruments) and 'does not undergo any quantitative alteration of value in the process of production' (317). Marx calls this 'constant' since the value of the investment in machinery and its replacement due to wear is, more or less, returned to the finished product in a calculable fashion. Because value can only be created by human labour, tools cannot create value. A piece of equipment simply transfers the value objectified within it to the object that it produces. We can make a machine go faster so that it transfers this value more quickly, or we can preserve a machine by using it slowly to prevent it from wearing out. But whether we use a machine quickly or slowly, it is 'strikingly clear that means of production never transfer more value to the product than they themselves lose during the labour process by the destruction of their own use-value' (312).

These costs are the required part of capital investment, since the capitalist must provide them for the labourers, who do not have their own tools. Yet because constant capital does not generate (surplus-)value, it can momentarily be left out of our consideration. Because the capitalist can calculate the amount of products that will come from raw material, there is neither any unexpected variable, nor any way to make surplus-value.

In contrast to constant capital, Marx defines 'variable capital' as the part of capital that does add value (317). Unsurprisingly, this capital comes from 'labour-power . . . [that] both reproduces the equivalent of its own value and produces an excess, a surplus-value, which may itself vary, and be more or less according to circumstances' (317). Variable capital is the cost of labour, the money invested in purchasing labour-power (wages) to make surplus-value (profit). Having determined that variable capital is the source of surplus-value, Marx now turns to the question of how fast can surplus-value be created; what determines its rate?

Chapter 9. The Rate of Surplus-Value

Section 1. The Degree of Exploitation of Labour-Power

Section 2. The Representation of the Value of the Product by Corresponding Proportional Parts of the Product

Capital consists of three parts, a formula that can be written as

$$C = (c + v) + s,$$

Capital = constant capital (equipment, materials) + variable capital (wages) + surplus-value (profit).

If we equate constant capital with zero, since the constant capital does not create value, the formula now appears as

$$C = v + s.$$

Marx defines *rate of surplus-value* as the 'ratio of surplus-value to the variable capital' (324) or surplus-value divided by variable capital (s / v). We can also understand this as the ratio of 'surplus labour' (the unpaid or underpaid labour that the capitalist takes from the labourer) to 'necessary labour' (what the worker needs to survive). This is different from the ratio Marx gives of surplus labour divided by the capital formed by the combined sum of constant and variable capital (s / (c + v)). Marx does not provide a name for this second ratio, but in the third volume of *Capital*, edited posthumously by Marx's close colleague Friedrich Engels, he calls the ratio of surplus labour to (total) capital the *rate of profit*, which is the surplus left over after having paid wages and the cost of machinery and materials.

The rate of profit differs from the rate of surplus-value in that the former also takes into account the investment costs of the equipment and materials that the capitalist must purchase to make commodities. Usually when we hear reports about business, they refer to the rate of profit rather than the rate of surplus-value. Marx focuses on the rate of surplus-value instead, thus ignoring the cost of equipment, because he wants first to draw our attention to the experience of labourers, his ideal readers, at this point, so that they have the terms to resist what has been their disempowering experience. He also says that when a scientist is trying to study a chemical process, she or he does not take into account the beakers and test tubes when explaining a chemical reaction. Similarly, Marx wants to explain a social reaction and while he will soon describe the importance of equipment and machinery, he will always and only do so insofar as they help us understand the experience of labourers as the important variable and the ways in which capitalist processes create social inequalities.

For instance, Marx explains that the rate of surplus-value is also the same as the fraction of surplus labour divided by necessary labour. When viewed in these terms, the rate of surplus-value is the 'degree of exploitation of labour-power by capital, or of the worker by the capitalist' (326). We now have a means of evaluating degrees of exploitation that can be used to assess 'various economic formations of society'. The greater the rate of surplus-value extracted from workers, the greater the rate of exploitation. Conversely, fairer societies will reduce the rate of surplus-value. This reduction does not mean that these societies are unproductive and create no or little exchange-value; it means that this value is not unfairly appropriated from the producers who never experience its benefits, either individually or socially, as might be the case with state-provided education, health care, housing, unemployment benefits, and other social welfare schemes.

To review the terms of this chapter, we can set out Marx's arguments like this:

The rate of surplus-value = surplus-value (profit) / variable capital (wages) = surplus labour ('exchangeable' labour,

labour for the capitalist) / necessary labour (useful labour, labour for the labourer) = **rate of exploitation**.

Section 3. Senior's 'Last Hour'

In this short, but complicated section, Marx challenges the argument, here attributed to the economist Nassau Senior, that an owner's profits will fall if the working day is shortened. Despite complaints by businessmen, Marx insists that reducing the time a labourer spends working does not necessarily reduce the rate of profit; after all, the work process might become more efficient so that more is produced in less time. Additionally, the rate of surplus-value is not calculated at the end of the day, but is ongoing throughout the entire workday. Since workers continuously deliver surplus-value as they work, they would still deliver surplus-value if they worked less, especially as they would use less raw materials (constant capital). The main motive for this section is how it prepares the next, much longer and more substantive one about the working day as the first historical phase of conflict between social classes in the workplace.

Chapter 10. The Working Day

In the last chapter, Marx presented his theory that surplus-value emerges from the gap between necessary and surplus labour. In this chapter, Marx examines how surplus-value is actually created in the sphere of production, in the first instance by lengthening the working day. His description about the working day is both general and historical. It is general in that this kind of exploitation is, as we shall see, a recurring feature of capitalism. It is historical as the coercion involved in prolonging work is particularly important during the early phase of capitalism's emergence and development. Marx calls this part of the volume 'The Production of Absolute Surplus-Value', in contrast to Part Four's 'The Production of Relative Surplus-Value'. He has not yet explained what he means by the absolute versus relative distinction, and it will not be until Chapter 12 that he clearly defines absolute surplus-value, the theme of this part, as 'that surplus-value which is produced by the lengthening of the working day' (432).

Section 1. The Limits of the Working Day

The first, most basic and cheapest way for capitalists to gain surplus-value from workers is to increase the overall length of the working day or shorten their breaks for eating and rest. This is the easiest tactic for bosses, since it does not require the risk of changing how work is done, which could fail to be more efficient and/or antagonize labourers, or the investment of spending on hiring more workers or buying new technology.

Remember that Marx argues that every worker needs to work a certain amount to pay for the necessities of life. Anything beyond this necessary labour is excess or surplus labour. You can probably sense the next step of his argument coming. If surplus labour creates surplus-value, then the capitalist who wants surplus-value will seek to increase surplus labour by forcing workers to labour longer than the time necessary for their needs and to work as hard as possible without any substantive increase in their wages. Marx uses an illustration to depict this point.

A————————B———C

The length from A to C is the total length of the working day. If A to B is the length of time for necessary labour, then the length from B to C is the period that creates surplus-value. If the length of A to C is increased by prolonging the working day, while the length of A to B remains the same, then the segment B to C widens, thus creating more surplus-value for the capitalist.

A————————B————————————C

As the magnitude of surplus-value increases, so, too, does the rate of exploitation (s / v).

Here the first of capitalism's intrinsic contradictions begins to surface. The increase of the working day reaches two limits. The first obstacle involves the physical limits: how long can the working day be extended before workers slow their productivity, as they become exhausted, sick, or even die? The second comes from the 'moral obstacles' that lead people to protest against overwork as something that brutalizes human 'intellectual and social requirements' (341), such as the time for family, friends, and self-reflection. Capitalists push their labourers to their human limits because they are driven to 'create surplus-value' by absorbing as much human vitality as possible. 'Capital is dead labour, which vampire-like, lives only by sucking living labour, and lives the more, the more labour it sucks' (342). Like all vampires, though, capital cannot stop itself from trying to kill the very humans that it needs to survive.

From the viewpoint of capitalists, who feel that they have 'bought' all of the worker's time, labourers are stealing potential surplus-value any time they are not working, such as when they take rest breaks. Although capitalists often preach saving, they hypocritically do not want workers to preserve their own labour. Marx again highlights the false notion that the market is a sphere of equality. Both workers and capitalists want to safeguard their own resources. The former want to preserve their strength so that they can continue working, while the latter want to preserve their rates of surplus-value and profit. At the conceptual level, we have an irresolvable confrontation,

> an antimony, of right against right, both equally bearing the seal of the law of exchange. Between equal rights, force decides. Hence, in the history of capitalist production, the establishment of a norm for the working day presents itself as a struggle over the limits of that day, a struggle between collective capital, i.e. the class of capitalists, and collective labour, i.e. the working class. (344)

For the first time in *Capital*, Marx explicitly raises the notion that the capitalist system is one engineered by class struggle. For Marx, the market place never operates peacefully, but is continually constituted through the struggle between workers and capitalists over the ownership of labour-power. When workers begin to use the same language of equal property rights that capitalists use to justify their own behaviour, then capitalists simply resort to violence. What now follows in the text are several sections on the history of social and political conflict over the length of the working day and the effort by workers to reclaim control over their labour-time.

Section 2. The Voracious Appetite for Surplus Labour.
Manufacturer and Boyar

Marx differentiates modern capitalist activity from the historical modes of production of earlier periods, especially slavery and serfdom, in terms of these periods' range and purpose in acquiring surplus labour. He admits that '[c]apital did not invent surplus labour' (344), for whenever 'a part of society possesses the monopoly of the means of production, the worker, free or unfree' gives extra labour-time beyond what is necessary for his survival. It does not matter if this property owner is an ancient Athenian, a Roman, a Norman baron, an East European noble (a Boyar), an American slave-owner, a modern landlord, or a capitalist.

> It is however clear that in any economic formation of society where the use-value rather than the exchange-value of the product predominates, surplus labour will be restricted by a more or less confined set of needs, and that no boundless thirst for surplus labour will arise from the character of production itself. (345)

While pre-capitalist societies did force labourers to create surplus-value, they often did so for non-market-oriented purposes and within certain predefined limits that placed a ceiling on work. Capitalists' unquenchable thirst for work-generated surplus-value breaks the customary social limits to the amount of labour that can be appropriated, for example, from a serf, who was overworked, but only within prescribed conditions.

Yet it must also be said that the distinction between these two different kinds of society erodes when they come into contact with one another, as capitalism often swallows up older patterns and recasts them for the purpose of profiteering. Overwork in ancient societies 'becomes frightful' as they move towards a fascination with money 'in the production of gold and silver. The recognized form of over-work here is forced labour unto death' (345). Likewise,

> as soon as people whose production still moves within the lower forms of slave-labour . . . are drawn into a world market dominated by the capitalist mode of production . . . the civilized horrors of over-work are grafted onto the barbaric horrors of slavery, serfdom etc. Hence the Negro labour in the southern states of the American Union preserved a moderately patriarchal character as long as production was chiefly directed to the satisfaction of immediate local requirements. But in proportion as the export of cotton became of vital interest to those states, the over-working of the Negro, and sometimes the consumption of his life in seven years of labour, became a factor in a calculated and calculating system. (345)

Even slavery in the United States becomes worse when cotton became a globally traded commodity. If a pre-capitalist society is brought into the trading relations of a capitalist one, then its labourers get the worst of both worlds: control by traditional hierarchies and the pressures of modern profiteering. With this comment, Marx draws our attention to how workers on the peripheries of the capitalist world system are usually treated worse than those in the metropolitan nations.

However, looked at from the other side, Marx also insists that workers in the dominant nations will be forced to sink to the level of slaves. Marx will consistently return to compare (black) slavery to (white) wage labour, since he insists that capitalism's growth and expansion always lower the quality of work and life conditions for labourers everywhere. For now he repeats that capitalists will constantly try to limit workers' break times for 'rest and refreshment' (351) to secretly prolong the working day, often by making them do labour, such as cleaning machines, after the official day is over. The capitalist's 'small thefts' and 'petty pilferings of minutes' along with a 'nibbling and cribbling at meal times' (352) all add to the surplus time and surplus-value that the labourer loses to his boss.

Section 3. Branches of English Industry Without Legal Limits to Exploitation

The 'drive towards the extension of the working day, and the werewolf-like hunger for surplus labour' (353), ultimately reaches the legal limits to the working day. In Marx's time, however, several industries, such as lacemaking, the pottery industry, match making, wallpaper making, baking, and the clothing industry, were able to escape these limits and push their workers 'unto death'. Marx cites the reports of official inspectors, which show that the long workdays in the dangerous work conditions of these industries resulted in their workers having lower life expectancies – especially child workers, who were highly susceptible to disease and physical collapse. For page after page, Marx simply recites what England's own government inspectors had to say about the sickening working and living conditions of the proletariat, including overcrowding in rotten rooms and adulterated food. Marx calls these modern workers 'white slaves' (365) because their conditions are similar to the horrors faced by African slaves in the New World. Just as slavers captured labour in faraway lands, the English metropolitan capitalists drew on hinterland regions like 'Scotland, the agricultural districts of the West of England, and – Germany' (361) for labour. Just as African slaves died from overwork, Marx cites the case of the young Mary Anne Walkley, a twenty-year-old English milliner, who died from exhaustion due to a lack of rest time while labouring.

Section 4. Day-Work and Night-Work. The Shift-System

The prolongation of the working day does not only involve the same set of workers labouring. Capitalists can also secure surplus-value by ensuring that the fixed capital of their machinery works continuously night and day, so that time is not lost in starting up and shutting down the equipment. This constant operation gives rise to the shift systems in factories, where the factories are kept running by teams of labourers. These shifts were frequently done by child labour, to the youths' educational and physical detriment.

Section 5. The Struggle for a Normal Working Day. Laws for the Compulsory Extension of the Working Day, from the Middle of the Fourteenth to the End of the Seventeenth Century

Section 6. The Struggle for a Normal Working Day. Laws for the Compulsory Limitation of Working Hours. The English Factory Legislation of 1833–64

Marx continues to compare the working conditions of European labourers with the dreadful conditions of

Africans captured and transported to the Americas as slaves, especially as the constant need for more labour led to agents looking for 'surplus population' in the agricultural regions of England. Because the only commodity that the capitalist desires is labour-power, his concern is how to get more of it, rather than the labourer's life conditions, especially as he believes either that there will always be more workers to be found or that they can be created by entering non- or weakly capitalist areas and forcing their inhabitants to sell their labour-power.

Against the pressures of overwork, English workers conducted a centuries-long struggle, going back to the fifteenth century, for laws that limited the working day. During the advent of large-scale industry in the last third of the eighteenth century, the working class finally won a rare legislative victory on the length of the working day. In response, capitalists immediately subverted the law's clauses by lowering wages, so that labourers now had to work longer hours to maintain the same weekly wage. Marx documents the manoeuvres between the English political parties on this issue until 1846–47, when the tide turned against workers. Restrictive tariffs were removed and free trade 'was proclaimed as the guiding star of legislation' (395), even as the working-class Chartist movement was at its high point. After working-class movements were shattered, in the aftermath of the failed European revolutions of 1848, capitalists simply ignored the laws, especially as they knew that if they were prosecuted, the cases would be ruled in their favour by judges from their own social class (401).

*Section 7. The Struggle for a Normal Working Day.
Impact of the English Factory Legislation on Other
Countries*

Marx begins this chapter by re-emphasizing that the production of surplus-value does not require any specific change in the mode of production, but he also foreshadows his subsequent argument about the relationship between technology and overwork by noting that the industries that most relentlessly prolonged the working day were the ones in which the means of production were revolutionized by inventions involving 'water-power, steam and machinery' (411). Workers' ability to resist longer working days weakens in the regions where capitalist practices are more developed and backed by technological advances (for reasons that he will explain later).

Conversely, workers' rights are paradoxically often more likely to be won in lesser-developed regions as backward regions can overleap more developed ones. Marx uses the example of the United States. As long as slavery existed, the presence of cheap labour kept down the wages of free labourers. Once slavery was abolished, American workers were suddenly able to gain an eight-hour working day, a right that English labourers had been unable to achieve. Marx does not explicitly comment on why this might have happened, but implicitly we can understand that the achievement of the shorter working day was a tactical compromise by capitalists in the face of possible cross-racial worker solidarity that might have overwhelmed the capitalists' control of the workforce. Similarly, though Marx does not explicitly treat the world market in this volume, we should notice how frequently he turns to highlighting the relationship between English workers and those labourers beyond England's national borders. Just as he began with the local instance of the commodity and then proceeded to unravel a larger network of unseen relations, Marx's focus on England similarly opens up the need to survey the effects of capitalist commodification on labour throughout the globe.

Chapter 11. The Rate and Mass of Surplus-Value

Marx summarizes some earlier points in this chapter as he shows that increasing the magnitude of value by enlarging the number of workers, as happens when production moves to day and night shifts, does not necessarily increase the rate of surplus-value. The rate of surplus-value is different from its scale and it can only be increased by exploiting workers more, 'i.e. the lengthening of the working day' through a 'coercive relation' that 'compels the working class to do more work than would be required by the narrow circle of its own needs' (424–5).

In capitalism's early phases, bosses do not actually transform working conditions, they just accept the pre-existing work relations and apply external pressure on labourers by making them work longer and harder within traditional patterns. Capital 'subordinates labour on the basis of the technical conditions within which labour has been carried up to that point in history. It does not therefore directly change the mode of production' (425). For this reason, Marx calls the profit made from 'the outside' of the working process *absolute surplus-value* and contrasts it in the next part with *relative surplus-value*. He calls the latter 'relative' because capitalists will begin to change the interior relations of the work process. As the strategy of gaining surplus-value 'absolutely' by making labourers work longer and harder begins to have diminishing returns, capitalists will begin to reshape the way in which work is done in order to regain the rate of surplus-value. How is this done?

Recall that Marx considers the working day to have a twofold nature, composed of necessary labour and surplus labour. In the last part, he considered that surplus-value could be created by increasing the length of the working day, so that as the length of necessary labour remains constant, the length of the surplus labour increases. In this chapter, Marx assumes the reverse. If the working day's length remains the same, then to increase surplus-value the price of necessary labour must fall.

To get more surplus-value from workers, capitalists could simply pay workers less, but this, too, has limits, since wages cannot ideally fall beneath the level that would sustain life. The price of a labourer can only fall if the commodities he requires for his (and his family's) sustenance and rejuvenation also become cheaper. But why would capitalists make commodities less expensive, if their primary goal is to increase the profit made through the sale of commodities? Marx provides two answers. Firstly, the constant competition among capitalists for control over the market place forces capitalists to lower the price of their goods to attract buyers. The capitalist gives up a certain amount of profit per item so that he can sell to a wider audience and achieve profit from an increased percentage of the market. A system that increases the volume of trade, however, requires either better equipment that can accelerate the production of commodities or a change in the work process that leads to more efficient production. Because acquiring new machinery involves investing in fixed capital and thus reducing profitability, capitalists generally delay paying for new equipment, and historically the first choice of capitalists was their attempt to break the artisan guild restrictions on how many workers and apprentices a craft master could employ – in other words, how much labour-power a master could acquire.

In the early modern period, the guilds limited the number of apprentices who could be trained to practise a craft. These restrictions prevented a cheapening overproduction of the commodities by a glut of craftsmen competing against one another within regionalized markets. Nonetheless, over time, single masters increasingly assumed command of larger numbers of apprentices. The increased ratio of apprentices to masters began to establish a split between manual and mental labour, as master artisans increasingly spent their time in *managing* the work process rather than either participating in it or training apprentices to learn how to replace them, and the increased number of apprentices meant that fewer would advance to the level of master craftsmen and become involved in making decisions about the labour process.

Capital's next part continues to track this developing gap between mental and manual labour, which Marx takes as indicating a new phase of capitalist activity. Before we turn to this, let us briefly review the claims of Part Three. Unpaid labour produces surplus-value. As the capitalist's first choice is to avoid investing in fixed capital and to get surplus-value in the cheapest and easiest way possible, he makes workers work longer for the same or less money than is conventional. Marx calls this the production of 'absolute surplus-value' because overwork has an absolute limit to it and because it does not get 'inside' the work process and the minds of labourers. Yet to advance, capitalism needs to revolutionize the work process itself, a move that leads to a focus on a different means of gaining surplus-value, the production of relative surplus-value.

Part Four: The Production of Relative Surplus-Value

Chapter 12. The Concept of Relative Surplus-value

In his discussion of absolute surplus-value, Marx assumed that the mechanism of the work process remained unchanged. If this is true, then lengthening the workday is the only means of creating surplus-value as capitalists 'take over the labour process in its given and historically transmitted shape and then simply . . . prolong its duration' (432). Once the physical, cultural, and legal limits to prolonging the workday have been reached, then the rate of surplus-value can only be increased by raising the labourer's productivity by changing the nature of the work process to 'shorten the labour-time necessary for the production of a commodity' and 'endow a given quantity of labour with the power of producing a greater quantity of use-value' (431). The labourer's productivity will increase either by 'an alteration in his tools or in his mode of working, or both' (431).

These two aspects, the 'technical and social conditions of the [work] process' (432), make up what Marx calls the *mode of production*. (The technical aspect alone is the *means of production*.) If the mode of production is revolutionized, 'the value of labour-power will fall, and the portion of the working day necessary for the reproduction of that value will be shortened' (432). By lowering the amount of time it takes to make a commodity, the commodity becomes cheaper, since it requires less (necessary) labour-time, and consequently the value of the labour-power that makes the commodity falls.

Relative surplus-value is the name Marx uses to categorize an increase in surplus-value resulting from a change in the process of work. It is 'relative' because it changes human relations *within* the work process, unlike what happens in absolute surplus-value, where older processes remain the same but have increased pressure placed on them. The difference between absolute and relative surplus-value can be looked at in terms of the desire to increase the amount of space that a building has for use. One way might simply be to build more floors on top of the pre-existing structure. At a certain point, the building will collapse because it cannot support the additional weight. Alternatively, we might decide to create more space by changing the building's infrastructure and the ways in which people move within it, perhaps by replacing spacious stairways with smaller elevators. Absolute surplus-value would be like the first option of adding to the pre-existing pattern: it simply latches on to the exterior of work processes. Relative surplus-value is like a virus that 'gets inside' a structure by inserting its DNA into the host and altering its genetic, interior structure. For this reason, Marx sees relative surplus-value as marking capitalism's substantive shift from being a marginal presence in early modern society to being the dominant one in the modern world. Indeed, capitalism's restructuring of production processes can arguably be listed as a key defining feature of modernity.

Because capitalists want to increase their *rate* of profit, they have 'an immanent drive, and a constant tendency, towards increasing the productivity of labour, in order to cheapen commodities and, by cheapening commodities, to cheapen the worker himself' (436–7). If the labour-time (the magnitude of value) needed to make an object decreases, then more productive labourers become cheaper to hire, since the amount of their labour invested in each commodity has fallen. Now we can solve the question of why capitalists, who want to create exchange-value, will reduce the exchange-value of their commodities. The rate of surplus-value increases only if the relative value of a particular key commodity – labour-power – is reduced.

The goal of capitalists is not really to increase the working day as a whole; they just want to increase the length of the part of the working day that delivers surplus-value. When the tactic of overwork reaches its limits and the length of the working day must remain static, then capitalists develop a more effective mode of production to decrease 'the labour-time necessary for the production of a definite quantity of commodities' (438), a move that reduces labour costs. Marx now turns to discuss the concrete, historical phases of this decrease.

Chapter 13. Co-operation

Marx says that capitalism 'only really begins' (439) when an individual capitalist 'simultaneously employs a comparatively large number of workers' so that

> the labour-process is carried on on an extensive scale and yields relatively large quantities of products. A large

number of workers working together, at the same time, in one place (or, if you like in the same field of labour), in order to produce the same sort of commodity under the command of the same capitalist, constitutes the starting-point of capitalist production. This is true both historically and conceptually. (439)

Capitalism proper starts by massifying labour-power.

Marx uses this change in the mode of production to differentiate two historical periods from one another. The earlier period, the 'Age of Handicrafts', is classified by the production of skilled artisans. The following period, running roughly from the 1550s to the 1830s, he calls the 'Age of Manufacture'. One difference between these two eras is that, in the Age of Handicrafts, the method of gaining surplus value was still dominated by the 'absolute' techniques of overwork. Another difference, which is 'purely quantitative' (439), is that the Age of Manufacture involves 'the greater number of workers simultaneously employed by the same individual capital. It is merely an enlargement of the workshop of the master craftsmen of the guilds' (439). The initial benefit of increasing the number of apprentice labourers that a single master has under his supervision is that it allows for the emergence of a more stable 'average labour-time' (441) among the various workers, removing 'individual differences, or "errors"' (440), and makes the work process more calculable and less prone to individual influences.

Even without changing the manner of production, the conglomeration of workers produces a 'revolution' in the work process through economies of scale. It costs less to build one workshop for 20 weavers than 10 workshops for two weavers. If workers are brought together, 'the value of a part of the constant capital falls' (442), meaning that the capitalist's operating cost for each individual worker decreases, since less money needs to be invested in the fixed capital costs of building and maintaining multiple worksites and less material and time is lost in transporting goods into, out of, and between different locations. Remember the equation, $C = (c + v) + s$. If the constant capital (c) decreases and the number of workers (v) remains unchanged, then the amount of surplus-value (s) will increase.

When 'numerous workers work side by side, in accordance with a plan, whether in the same process, or in different but connected processes', Marx calls this form of labour 'co-operation' (443). Co-operation alone creates a 'new productive power, which is intrinsically a collective one' (443). Marx believes that because humans have a natural desire for community, 'mere social contact' makes workers more productive: their contact with one another motivates them to work harder, often through rivalry, and more effectively than they would if they worked either alone or in small groups. In this way, it is workers themselves, rather than their bosses, who push each other to do more work. Another benefit of co-operation for capitalists is that the time necessary for the completion of a commodity can be shortened as large groups work on the same task, especially in cases where work has to be done quickly lest the raw materials will be lost (as happens when harvesting a crop). Co-operation also allows 'work to be carried on over a large area', especially involving large-scale projects such as building irrigation and water-control systems or trans-portation networks, like 'canals, roads and railways' (446), which would otherwise be impossible for a small group to complete. Thus, co-operation 'while extending the scale of production . . . renders possible a relative contraction of its arena'. The 'simultaneous restriction of space and extension of effectiveness' (446) allows for the reduction of wasted time and loss of materials. Co-operation allows capitalism to operate on a much greater scale than it had previously been able to do.

Unfortunately for workers, co-operation often makes them lose their prior individuality, as their work conditions fuse them into a new, more collective, identity – especially as the products of co-operation do not seem to belong to any individual worker. Because it is harder for individual labourers to determine their own exact contribution, labourers can only identify themselves as part of a group. Consequently, they begin to feel alienated from their own sense of self, as they do not seem to create any value by themselves. In this way, we can also see how commodities can become increasingly fetishized through a change in the mode of production. When large numbers of workers are involved in making the commodity, it becomes easier for even the labourer to think that the created surplus-value is a feature of the object itself, rather than the result of many individuals working together. But if workers seem to lose out to commodities, they are in reality losing out to an increasingly more powerful capitalist. As workers become 'incorporated' into this larger mass, the resulting 'working organism . . . appears as a power which capital possesses by its nature – a productive power inherent in capital' (451). We could say that this is the fetish of co-operation, where it looks as if it is the capitalist's organization, rather than the workers themselves, that creates this new power. Furthermore, the extra efficiency made by the workers themselves through co-operation appears like 'a power which capital possesses by its nature . . . inherent in capital'; it 'develops as a free gift to capital' (451).

While co-operation increases the average social labour, 'as a general rule, workers cannot co-operate without being brought together' (447) by a single capitalist or capitalist firm who can afford to pay all these workers and invest in the fixed capital for the material to house and occupy the workers. Not only are there fewer capitalists who have the finances to employ large numbers of workers, it also becomes harder for a single capitalist to organize the work. To gain the benefits of workers' co-operation, a capitalist needs to develop a new method of managing this larger group of labourers. Consequently, in order for a master craftsman to become a capitalist, he must increasingly spend his time organizing work, rather than participating in it. He must take 'command in the field of production' (448). 'The work of directing, superintending and adjusting becomes one of the functions of capital, from the moment that the labour under capital's control becomes co-operative' (449).

The transformation of the master from being a more experienced labourer to a supervisor of others substantively changes the nature of work for those who continue to labour. If humans are distinguished from animals by a mental and manual division, then this separation is blurred when capitalists increasingly monopolize the 'thinking' aspect of work and limit their labourers to simply being 'hands'.

Yet in a dialectical fashion, the creation of larger numbers of workers also poses a new obstacle to capitalists in the form of increased worker resistance. By bringing workers to labour together, the capitalist allows them to gain a new knowledge of and solidarity with each other as workers, in ways that labourers who worked in small-scale workshops lacked. Individuals who are brought together to work alongside each other generally gain a group consciousness and solidarity previously unavailable to isolated artisans. These collectivized workers encourage each other to resist the capitalist's mastery, a resistance which is necessary: for as 'co-operation extends its scale' and generates worker solidarity, the process of managing workers becomes increasingly punitive.

A new form of despotism arrives as the capitalist, who is increasingly unable himself to survey the entire field of work,

> hands over the work of direct and constant supervision of the individual workers and groups of workers to a special kind of wage-labourer. An industrial army of workers under the command of a capitalist requires, like a real army, officers (managers) and N.C.O.s (foremen, overseers), who command during the labour process in the name of capital. The work of supervision becomes their established and exclusive function. (450)

The cost of supervising workers in a military fashion now gets treated as constant capital or the fixed costs of production, where police-like management appears as necessary a cost for the capitalist as the raw materials for the actual production of commodities.

This chapter thus ties together two of *Capital*'s main themes: the problem of what seems to be self-expanding value (fetishism) and the loss of human control (alienation, objectification) to the inorganic system. These two effects converge to find a form of appearance in the new status of the commodity, which seems to create value by itself. Increasingly, we understand why Marx wanted to begin with discussing commodities rather than how labourers are exploited: he wants to show how what we see in the market place is related to the experience of those in the sphere of production, even if this experience is obscured by capitalist interests.

Keeping the need for historical specificity in mind, Marx says that the act of bringing large masses of workers together in one space is not by definition a capitalist practice, since this conglomeration of labourers happened in the building of 'gigantic structures erected by the ancient Asiatics, Egyptians, Etruscans, etc.' (451). Co-operation also took place 'at the beginning of human civilizations, among hunting peoples' and appears sporadically in the Middle Ages and in colonial slave plantations. Historically, these forms of pre-capitalist co-operation were developed 'in opposition to peasant agriculture and independent handicrafts, whether in guilds or not' (452). Capitalist co-operation is different from these earlier forms, which mainly rely on slave labour, because 'the capitalist form presupposes from the outset the free wage-labourer who sells his labour-power to capital' (452). In this way, 'from the standpoint of the peasant and the artisan, capitalist co-operation does not appear' (453) immediately as a threat to farmers and the guilds, who were initially more concerned about falling back in status to the serf-like conditions of feudalism than with the proletarian-izing conditions of capitalism.

The implication of Marx's comment here is that resistance to capitalism will initially occur within urban manufactories, even though the first instances of capitalism's change in labour relations occurred in the countryside, as Marx explains later. On the other hand, there was a reason why peasants and artisans did not recognize the effects of capitalist co-operation, for while 'co-operation remains the fundamental form of the capitalist mode of production . . . simple co-operation' has often existed without beginning the irreversible process to capitalism. Yet the 'simultaneous employment of a larger number of wage-labourers in the same labour process . . . forms the starting point of capitalist production. This starting point also coincides with the birth of capital itself' (453). Once this transitional form appears, it remains fundamental to the capitalist mode of production, and 'in its simple shape it continues to appear as one particular form alongside the more developed ones' (454).

Chapter 14. The Division of Labour and Manufacture

Section 1. The Dual Origins of Manufacture

The introduction of co-operation represents a gradually increasing move towards capitalism. Marx now turns to the first full-blown era of capital, the 'Age of Manufacture', which 'extends, roughly speaking, from the middle of the sixteenth century to the last third of the eighteenth century' (455).

Manufacture originates in two ways. The first is the aforementioned aspect of simple co-operation's 'assembling together in one workshop, under the control of a single capitalist, . . . workers belonging to various independent handicrafts, through whose hands a given article must pass on its way to completion' (455). The massification of workers within one space also allows for the possibility of another kind of co-operation, involving the division of labour that goes into making a commodity. An important change takes place when different kinds of craftsmen are brought together to do one aspect of a work process dedicated to a single commodity, such as when locksmiths are brought to work in a manufactory only to make locks for carriages. When skilled artisans repeat one process over and over again, 'they gradually lose the habit and therefore the ability, of carrying on their old trade in all its ramifications' (455). As crafts workers do not practise the full range of their skills, they progressively become a 'partial' or specialized worker. Although work is still done by artisans, this narrowing of skills further increases the division of mental and manual labour. As craftsmen become more like cogs within a larger process, their expertise erodes in ways that make them increasingly unable to work outside of the capitalist-controlled manufactory.

A second defining feature of manufacture is the further breakdown of artisan skills when labourers are hired to do smaller segments of the process that makes a commodity. 'Instead of each man being allowed to perform all the various operations in succession, these operations are changed into disconnected, isolated ones, carried on side by side', a division that 'ossifies into a systematic division of labour' (456). Here locksmiths might only each make a part of the lock, rather than the whole lock itself. In this way, the commodity no longer belongs to any single worker, but is the product of many different labourers.

The specialization and fragmentation of the work process undermines artisan authority and the autonomy of the older guilds in two ways. Firstly, by bringing many different crafts together (this is the condensation of the work arena), craftsmen must now work according to the schedule of other crafts. They lose their old independence and ability to determine their work and rest schedule. Secondly, the 'decomposition of a handicraft into its different partial operations' (457) makes work more and more robotic. Segmentation of the work process 'deskills' the labourer, as these segments could increasingly be done by those who lack years of artisan training.

Section 2: The Specialized Worker and His Tools

Looking at the matter more closely, we see that if a worker repeatedly does only one aspect of the work process, he learns how to do it faster, so that he (and for Marx this is still a 'he', for reasons that he will explain later) has to spend less energy on the task. This self-created efficiency unwittingly helps to produce more surplus-value for the capitalist. Yet, in the absence of the labourer streamlining the workflow, the capitalist will do it for him. For even if the traditional artisan only makes part of a commodity, he often changes place in the shop – even if this is only moving from one side of a work bench to another – and must handle different tools. These actions 'lose' time the labourer could otherwise spend actually transferring value into commodities. A specialized worker who remains stationary doing one thing over and over again can now use this time 'productively', that is in producing surplus-value for the capitalist. Capitalists obviously want to find ways in which labourers become less free to move about and they will look to segment the work process whenever possible in order to make the worker more static.

Traditionally the skills of creating things were safeguarded by guild exclusions and hereditary castes. The guilds prevented anyone who had not undergone years of training in specialized skills from working (or learning) a craft. Similarly, in some societies, certain trades, like tanning, were limited to a social group that you were born into. Both methods create protective limits that prevent wages from being lowered, since workers who have been specially trained by a protective group of masters or elders know that they cannot easily be replaced and that few commodities will get produced without their consent. Capitalists overcome these obstacles by developing specialized tools for each task that makes it easier to create a commodity without strength, dexterity or expertise. The work process is broken down into segments that ideally can each be done with a single tool. 'Manufacture is characterized by the differentiation of the instruments of labour . . . the manufacturing period simplifies, improves and multiplies the implements of labour by adapting them to the exclusive and special functions of each kind of worker' (460–1). Once tools have become so specialized, the process can be made more efficient as each worker saves time by optimally using a single tool to do only one task over and over again. With a tool for each task, the capitalist no longer needs recalcitrant highly skilled workers who might interfere with the production of surplus-value.

Section 3. The Two Fundamental Forms of Manufacture – Heterogeneous and Organic

There are two 'fundamental forms of articulation', the bringing together within a single process, that help transform manufacturing in ways that point to its revolution in the next phase, the 'Age of Large-Scale Machinery'. The first form is 'heterogeneous manufacture', where many workers make parts of an object, which are later brought together and assembled to create the finished commodity. This method does not achieve the maximum benefits of economies of scale as the work process is scattered all over the workshop. The second is a 'perfected form', what Marx calls 'organic manufacture', when articles go 'step by step through a series of processes' like an assembly line. This form is more profitable since it 'lessens the space by which the various phases of production are separated from each other. The time taken in passing from one stage to another is shortened, and so is the labour by means of which these transitions are made' (463). As the work process has become 'simultaneous and contiguous in its space', all the various workers become a 'collective worker, formed from the combination of the many specialized workers' (464).

When work is broken down into small, simultaneously operating interdependent units, it becomes increasingly easier for capitalists to predict how long it will take to make a commodity, since the perfected form of manufacture 'creates a continuity, a uniformity, a regularity, an order, and even an intensity of labour, quite different from that found in an independent handicraft or even in simple co-operation' (465). By turning the work process into interlocking segments, manufacture begins also to understand what proportions of labour tasks are required to make the entire process continue without interruptions. For instance, if one worker in one segment can prepare twice as much as one worker can do in the next segment, then the capitalist recognizes that he needs twice as many workers for that second segment to prevent the first worker from waiting around or producing too many goods that then have to be stock-piled, thus making them unproductive and increasing the need for the fixed capital of storage costs.

Once these proportions have been calculated for one industry, they can be used to work out what is needed for other kinds of manufacture as well. The effects of this are twofold. Firstly, previously autonomous kinds of manufacturing become more and more interlinked in ways that help in the transfer of capitalist practices from one workplace to another. Secondly, the worker solidarity that was gained through co-operative work and the creation of a collective worker identity is undermined. With the introduction of specialized tools, manufacturers create a hierarchy of jobs. At the top of this pyramid are the workers with skills that cannot yet be replaced with tools because these tasks still require dexterity or precision. These 'elite' labourers often view lesser-skilled workers with contempt, mainly because they fear that one day they could also be as deskilled and vulnerable.

As workers are deskilled through segmentation of work and the proliferation of tools, they require less training, education, and practice. We can now recall how the commodities a worker needs can be cheapened without reducing the profit of the capitalists who make commodities. Remember that education was considered by Marx as part of a worker's necessary labour, much like food. If workers do not need training, which the capitalist paid for in the higher wages given to the more experienced workers who trained the younger ones, then their necessary labour costs decrease. Since workers no longer have to pay for education, even if done in terms of apprentice service, the cost that a labourer's necessary labour must acquire goes down. These reductions, in turn, allow for wages to be reduced and consequently the rate of surplus-value increases. The division of labour in manufacture creates

How to Read Marx's *Capital*

profit by reorganizing the work process through time-saving segmentation and aggravating the manual versus mental labour division so that 'management' can deskill labourers, thus creating the conditions enabling them to lower the wages of labourers, who now need less training.

Section 4. The Division of Labour in Manufacture, and the Division of Labour in Society

As we have seen, almost every time that Marx makes an argument about a feature of capitalism, he tries to illustrate the ways in which these features are specific to capitalist activity, even if aspects of these features have appeared before in history. In this section, Marx shows that the division of labour in manufacture is different from divisions of labour in society, partly because the former restlessly seeks to increase its domain.

The division of labour in society first occurs when work is divided between men and women and/or adults and the young. This kind of division occurs when 'tribes' increasingly come into contact with each other to trade commodities. When groups routinely trade, they often create a division of tasks, so that the group can continue to make the use-values that it needs to survive as well as exchangeable commodities. The most basic 'foundation' for every division of labour beyond these early ones is 'the separation of town from country' (472). In passing, Marx says that 'the whole economic history of society is summed up in the movement of this antithesis' between the urban and the rural. We can think of this not simply as a division within one country, but also as a way to describe international divisions between the West and the developing 'Third

World'. Marx says that the distinction between the city and the countryside is 'relative' so that a 'thinly populated country, with well-developed means of communication, has a denser population than a more numerously populated country with badly developed means of communication. In this sense, the northern states of the U.S.A. for instance, are more thickly populated than India' (473).

Despite the surface similarities between the divisions of labour that take place 'in the interior of society' and those taking place in the 'interior of a workshop' (474), these divisions are different, not only in degree, but also in kind. In society, the divisions of labour relate to subjects who make an entire commodity. In manufacture, 'the specialized worker produces no commodities' (475), since he now only generates a *fraction* of a commodity. The division of labour in society occurs through the buying and selling between 'different branches of industry', while the division of labour in a manufactory is controlled by a single capitalist entity planning the entire work process. The division of labour in society brings together 'independent producers of commodities', while workers in a manufactory lack this freedom, as they create commodities only by trading their labour-power in advance of their wages.

Historically, whenever a group or society grew so much that there were not enough resources for all, this tension was resolved by forming a new village or colony. The extra population was hived off in a peaceful manner to prevent increasing demand for group resources from being destroyed by intense internecine competition. The European guilds tried to achieve something like this regulation of resource by limiting access to crafts training, and the guilds fought the attempt to break this control by 'merchants' capital, the only free form of capital which confronted them. A merchant could buy every kind of commodity, but he could not buy labour as a commodity' (479). While guilds created divisions of labour by policing the boundary lines between different trades (such as leather-working and tanning), their inflexibility also guarded against the breakdown of these skills. The craft guilds also tried to prevent masters from taking on more apprentices so that workshops would not get large enough to comprehensively segment the work process. In many ways, capitalist manufacture could not rise until the defensive power of the guilds had been diminished.

The division of labour in manufacture is clearly a capitalist-driven form of labour differentiation, one driven by the need for incessant valorization. Yet Marx raises a question that he will pursue over the next several sections and chapters: how does the division of labour in manufacture (the specialized labour in the factory) relate to the division of labour in society? How do capitalist industrial relations spread through non-capitalist sections of a society?

Section 5. The Capitalist Character of Manufacture

Reviewing some of his arguments, Marx claims that capitalist manufacture not only 'subjects the previously independent worker to the discipline and command of capital, but creates in addition a hierarchical structure amongst the workers themselves' (481) by dividing the work process into gradations of skilled and unskilled tasks. Even the skilled labourers, however, become 'mutilated' as they are forced to give up the total range of their skills and made ignorant of what they once knew. Marx notes that many manufacturers even preferred to 'employ semi-idiots' who would not be able to learn the 'trade secrets' of the work process (483) and then demand higher wages. The harm to workers resulting from the division of labour was even recognized by Adam Smith, who saw that the tedium of repetitive work 'naturally corrupts the courage of [the worker's] mind' (483). While Smith felt that it was necessary to counterbalance this by providing greater education for labourers, to replace what they had lost through manufacture, Smith's followers had no such scruples, given their belief that education would only re-empower labourers and better enable their resistance against the capitalist's desire for profit.

Marx believes that the division of labour in manufacture creates a particular 'industrial pathology' (484) that damages workers both physically and mentally. Manufacture increases the 'socially productive power of labour for the benefit of the capitalist instead of the worker'; disables the individual worker; produces new conditions for the domination of capital over labour; and is a more 'refined and civilized means of exploitation', in the sense of not relying overtly on forcing the labourer to work harder or longer (486). Yet while overwork's trauma could be repaired with proper rest and refreshment, the damage created by manufacture permanently disables the worker as it produces a social experience that is irreversible for the individual, especially in the loss of past skills and an experience of independence. Because academic liberal political economy emerged simultaneously with the rise of manufacture, academic writers took capitalism's assumptions as normal and true throughout history. They almost literally could not understand the older economic writing of the Greeks, for instance, because these authors emphasized the production of use-values rather than exchange-values.

Instead, modern political economists took capitalism as the norm and consequently had trouble perceiving its historical appearance and internal transformations or delays.

For instance, capitalism was not able to appear spontaneously or without resistance by workers. Throughout the long manufacturing period, capitalists were not able to dictate changes with complete authority, and it took nearly 300 years for capital to seize control of the work process. Manufacturers often had to move 'from one country to another with the emigration or immigration of workers' (490), if workers moved to regions where they might regain self-determination, often by looking for land that they could farm. Even with the division of labour, the 'narrow technical basis' of familiar technologies limited the profit that could be created, because it was often hard to develop processes that could replace skilled workers. However, just as overwork reaches a limit that begins to reduce the rate of surplus-value, so too does manufacturing. Only with the industrial revolution, beginning with the rise of machinery in the last third of the eighteenth century, could capitalists finally 'abolish the role of the handicraftsman as the regulating principle of social production' (491). As capitalism revolutionizes the mode of production in order to continue the restless rate of accumulation, Marx now turns to the next historical phase, marked by machinery's ability to create even larger sites of industrial production.

Before we continue, let us take a moment to review Marx's historical periodization (see Table 1).

Keep these features of capitalism in mind: capital shifts the possession of power (skills, labour-power) from people (labourers) to objects, which are really the possessions of the traders in commodities; the material nature of a traded

Table 1 The Ages of Capitalism

Period	Dates	Mode of value creation	Method for creating surplus-value
Era of handicrafts	15th c.–mid 16th c.	Absolute surplus-value	Lengthening the working day
Era of manufacture	Mid 16th c.–18th c.	Relative surplus-value	Co-operation; specialized labour
Era of industry	Last third of 18th c.–1860s	Relative surplus-value	Machinery (automation); large-scale industry

commodity is irrelevant to the capitalist, who is only interested in a commodity's ability to generate profit; and when workers resist modes of creating profit, capital adapts new strategies to overcome these limits, usually by revolutionizing the existing mode of production.

We now turn to *Capital*'s longest and perhaps most memorable chapter.

Chapter 15. Machinery and Large-Scale Industry

Section 1. The Development of Machinery

Marx now turns to describing the period that many consider to be the classic age of capitalist modernity, machinery, and large-scale industry in the factory – the industrial era that started in the last third of the eighteenth century. Although Marx will focus on the historical changes that machinery introduces, he also cautions us that he is 'concerned here only with broad and general characteristics, for epochs in the history of society are no more separated from each other by strict and abstract lines of demarcation than are geological epochs' (492). There is no clear division between different periods, since social history often overlaps and blurs differences, even while it creates them. Sometimes older practices continue or return long after new ones have been introduced.

An example of one return involves the purpose of machinery. In 'large-scale industry . . . the instruments of labour are the starting point' (492) for these changes. While many think that new technology is invented to reduce the overall amount of time we need to work in order to finish a set task, Marx argues that this is not the aim under capitalism.

> Like every other instrument for increasing the productivity of labour, machinery is intended to cheapen commodities and, by shortening the part of the working day in which the worker works for himself, to lengthen the other part, the part he gives to the capitalist for nothing. The machine is a means for producing surplus-value. (492)

This surplus-value is created by the return to overwork. For new machinery always tends to increase the length of the working day even as it decreases the amount of time required for the completion of any single task. Think about how recent technology (computers, mobile phones) has made long-distance communication much easier and reduced the time we previously spent waiting for information or goods to arrive. Rather than allowing us to leave work earlier, since the job has been done more quickly, the new technologies have had the reverse effect of increasing the length of what we consider the permissible working day. This example highlights Marx's argument regarding technology, which is that its larger purpose under capitalism is not to ease human existence, but to facilitate its exploitation.

To understand how the nineteenth century creates the conditions for the return of centuries-old techniques, we need to ask: What is a machine and how is it different from the Age of Manufacture's tools? Marx writes that in his time mathematicians, mechanical experts, and English economists saw no 'essential difference' between a tool and a machine; they just called a tool a simple machine and a machine a complex tool. Marx finds this a worthless explanation because it does not take historical development into account. Others say that the difference is that a tool is powered (its 'motive power', what puts it into motion) by humans, while a machine is driven by natural forces, like animals, water, or wind. Marx considers this a silly explanation, since it defines an ancient plough driven by oxen as a machine. Clearly animal power was used long before the advent of modern machinery.

Marx looks at the problem differently by defining a machine as having three different parts: a motor mechanism, a transmitting mechanism, and a tool or 'working mechanism'. He defines the motor mechanism as 'the driving force of the mechanism as a whole' (494), like an engine. The transmitting mechanism 'regulates the motion, changes its form where necessary . . . and distributes it among the working machines [the tools]'. It involves the 'fly-wheels, shafting, toothed wheels, pulleys, straps, ropes, bands, pinions and gearing of the most varied kind' (494) that transfer power from the motor mechanism to other parts of the machine. The last aspect, the tool, is what the 'industrial revolution of the eighteenth century' changed with manufacture's proliferation of tools.

A machine is different from a simple tool not because it is composed of newly invented tools or has a non-human power source, but because of the way in which these tools and power are systematized so as to disempower their human minders. While humans used tools in the age of manufacturing, in the age of machinery, humans are used by machines. It has always been the case that there has been the tendency to replace human motive power with that of wind or animals, but these implements do not create 'any revolution in the mode of production' (496). The change has not occurred because humans are no longer the motive power, but because they are no longer the ones that organize the machine's internal operations. In other words, humans no longer control the *relationship* between the motive power, the transmitting mechanism, and tools: the machine itself seems in charge.

Because machines now do the 'internal' work of organizing production, they are wrongly seen as having an artificial intelligence. As Marx later suggests, this is the 'fetish' of the machine age that will confuse a machine's operation with human premeditation. Even when new technologies are invented, they have to wait until humans decide how these inventions should be used. For instance, Marx notes that the steam engine, invented at the end of the 1600s, did not make any impact until 1770, in the early moments of the industrial age, because the Age of Manufacture's disestablishment of skilled workers had not become fully enshrined. The mode of production, in this case that of manufacture, has to change before an invention can take hold. New technology does not make changes in advance of a social alteration. Yet once a machine has been introduced within a systematized work process, it can hugely amplify and accelerate these changes in ways that make it seem as if machinery initiated the changes, without consideration for human planning or desires (in this case for profit). When machinery revolutionizes the motive power and transmitting mechanism, these now seem to have 'an independent form, entirely emancipated from human strength' and consciousness (499).

We 'have now to distinguish the co-operation of a number of machines of one kind from a complex system of machinery' (499). A machine is not just something that can simultaneously operate more tools, like ten looms at once, than might a human. A machine articulates different kinds of tools and operations, involving a 'combination of different tools', into a whole mechanism (500). Where an old factory might have many smaller machines working next to one another, a 'machine' in large-scale industry works as one gigantic organism.

In manufacture, a tool was developed to replicate a worker's skill; it had as its model the movements of the human body. In machinery, the human element is entirely absent. No such adaptation to humans needs to occur, since the work process is entirely automated. This is a world run by objects for objects, where humans seem an awkward interference. Humans now have to adapt to the ways in which machines work, rather than using specialized tools that mimicked what humans had previously done. If manufacturers had to learn how to co-ordinate different human workers, the same is true with machinery, so that an 'articulated system' of machines can arise. If the division of labour was the main task for capitalist manufacture, then the opposite takes place in the mechanized factory, where capitalists now try to understand how these parts can be fused back together by machines.

The name Marx gives for a 'system of machinery' as soon as it becomes a conglomerated, 'self-acting prime mover' is 'automaton' (502). The apparatus appears automatic as it seems as if the machine is running itself. Because the automaton is massively more powerful than people, it appears to invert power relations between human subjects and their objects, especially as machines do not reach the same limitations of human exhaustion and weakness that put a limit to the tactic of absolute surplus-value (lengthening the working day). Once the process of machinery's organization begins, it develops much more quickly than was the case with the invention of tools in the Age of Manufacture, especially as machinery is now constantly improved and increased to become even larger, a 'mechanical monster whose body fills whole factories, and whose demonic power . . . finally bursts forth in the fast and feverish whirl of its countless working organs' (503). As the capitalist factory combines different machines, it seems like a Titan threatening to crush the human ants that get in its way.

After outgrowing the factory, machinery forces its way into other fields. 'The transformation of the mode of production in one sphere of industry necessitates a similar transformation in other spheres' (505) as it connects different industries together in ways that were not previously attempted. 'Thus machine spinning made machine weaving necessary, and both together made a mechanical and chemical revolution compulsory in bleaching, spinning and dyeing' (505). This is especially true in 'communication and transport' (506) where mechanization allows for an acceleration of capital's movement, particularly involving financial transactions, throughout the world market.

Notice how Marx's description of industry parallels the sequence of events in manufacture, but this time with machines, in order to reverse the gains made by labourers in the prior phase. If manufacture created a collective labourer who could resist the human capitalist through strikes and unions, the proletariat now faces an inanimate 'collective machine', which seems to be winning all the time. Machinery's replacement of humans is especially apparent with regards to specialized skills, since machines have their own 'prime mover' (506) that maintains perfect control over the process in ways that no human eye or hand could possibly hope to match. In manufacture, the focus of the system was still 'subjective', as it concentrated on rearranging human labour. In large-scale industry, it is entirely 'objective', as it looks to rearrange machinery.

Section 2. The Value Transferred by the Machinery to the Product

After describing the terrors of machinery, Marx turns back to the question of value transfers and exchanges to see why capitalists seem to allow the machine such authority. The answer is not immediately obvious, since it seems to forgo the advantage of the prior period, where 'the productive forces resulting from co-operation and the division of labour cost capital nothing. They are natural forces of social labour' (508). The resulting profits come from human, variable capital that is the source of surplus-value. On the other hand, the constant capital of machinery creates no new value, but simply transfers the value that went into making it to the commodity. A machine 'never adds more value than it loses, on the average, by depreciation' (509). If machines do not make new value, why would the capitalist invest in them? Any saving of labour that comes from machines is simply value that has been spent on research costs to invent the machine and the production costs of actually making the different parts of the machine. 'All that has taken place is a displacement of labour' (513) in producing a machine; there has been no real *creation* of value.

A machine becomes more 'productive', however, solely by the amount of 'human labour-power it replaces' (513), as it allows for a single worker to do the work of what previously took many to do. 'Before Eli Whitney invented the cotton gin in 1793, the separation of the seed from a pound of cotton cost an average day's labour. By means of his invention it became possible for one black woman to clean 100 lb. a day' (514). While a machine has embedded within it the value that it took to make it, 'the labour objectified in it is still much smaller in quantity than the living labour it replaces' (515). As machines allow fewer workers to produce more, the amount of labour-power (variable capital) that the capitalist must buy decreases, even as the amount of surplus-value created by each of the remaining workers increases. Consequently, the rate of surplus-value increases, due to the presence of fewer labourers in total. On the other hand, if human labour-power is so cheap, capitalists will continue to exploit it. 'In England women are still occasionally used instead of horses for hauling barges' (517) because the labour-power of women is less expensive than what it would cost to purchase, house, and feed the animals.

Section 3: The Most Immediate Effects of Machine Production on the Worker

While machinery allows a worker to wield more mechanical power, it also functions psychologically in breaking down the male labourers' will to resist the factory owner's commands. Capitalists accomplish this by allowing women and children to work in the factory, since machinery's operation does not require either the strength or the years of craft training that was previously necessary.

As machinery makes 'muscular power' less necessary, the adult male's labour can be cheapened in several ways as he works alongside women and children. Firstly, if the entire family labours in the factory, then the man finds that the cost of his labour-power can be depreciated because the amount of necessary labour that he needs is now spread throughout the family. If the man is no longer the only one working, then he does not have to be paid as much as previously, since the entire family will work to achieve the necessities that only the man worked for before. From the capitalist's perspective, the ability to exploit the labour of a family group, rather than just an individual, means that there will be a huge jump in the level of surplus-value produced.

The introduction of women into the workplace also has a deskilling effect that benefits capital, as women who previously saved money by providing certain basic needs, such as breastfeeding children, cooking, weaving, and sewing, now purchase these needs in the form of the commodities of milk, clothing, and food. As women lose their knowledge of domestic 'crafts', they lose the self-sufficiency that cushioned them from having to purchase these commodities in the market place.

As women move from being producers of their family's use needs to being producers of surplus-value and consumers, they inadvertently introduce the capitalist social system into the household. A similar appropriation of the private family occurs as machinery 'also revolutionizes, and quite fundamentally, the agency through which the capital-relation is formally mediated, i.e. the contract between the worker and the capitalist' (519). Now that the capitalist can buy the labour-power of women and children, the male worker turns his family into objects that can be sold to the capitalist. Machinery not only alienates the worker, but it also forces him to alienate his family as well. The worker 'sells wife and child. He has become a slave-dealer' (519). Since women and children customarily get paid less than men (as a legacy of the pre-capitalist patriarchal divisions of labour in society), technical innovation allows the factory's division of labour to incorporate older social divisions, by using gender and generational differences for the purposes of making profit.

The male labourer's assertion of control over his wife and children also helps to project the logic of capitalism throughout society, making male labourers now see the factory as a site of gender and generational confrontation (with labouring-class women and children) rather than one of class struggle (against the bosses). The effect of machinery's introduction of 'women and children to the working personnel, at last breaks the resistance which the male workers had continued to oppose to the despotism of capital throughout the period of manufacture' (526), as workers turn their energies against other workers rather than their bosses. While male labourers assert their rights as 'men', they forget that this defence of masculinity works to the benefit of the bosses. Although this is not mentioned by Marx, something similar can be said about how racism in the workplace also splinters what ought to be solidarity among workers.

The damage to labourers is physical as well as social. The effect of machinery's cheapening of labour's value is that they must compromise, in turn, the basic conditions of life. The rise of machinery creates a terrible environment for labourers, and Marx spends pages describing the 'insufficient nourishment', inadequate housing, and horrible life conditions for labourers, which increase their death rate and 'moral degradation', as workers receive less education and increasingly rely on painkilling drugs to get through the trauma of their everyday lives.

In their weakened state, workers also find that machinery creates the conditions for the working day to be lengthened all over again, thus reintroducing a stream of absolute surplus-value. Capitalists want their machinery to remain in constant motion, lest it deteriorate, through either lack of use or the apparatus's increasing obsolescence. For

> in addition to the material wear and tear, a machine also undergoes . . . a moral depreciation. It loses exchange-value, either because machines of the same sort are being produced more cheaply than it was, or because better machines are entering into competition with it. (528)

A capitalist worries that his competitors are going to be able to buy more recent and efficient technology while he is stuck with an increasingly obsolete machine. Because the capitalist fears that his equipment is not going to be as good as the more recent inventions, he tries to get back the value of his investment as quickly as possible by increasing the working day and through uninterrupted use of the machinery. The return to overwork reminds us that aspects of each earlier phase in capitalist development can always be recalled if the conditions are right.

To maximize usage of his machinery, the capitalist also insists that labourers take fewer breaks from their work. These are costly to him, and meanwhile his competitors introduce better equipment, while he has not yet paid off the investment in his older machinery. Consequently, the capitalist intensifies labour conditions by increasing the machinery's operating speed and the number of machines that a single worker has to supervise. Not only has the working day increased, it has become all the more hard and exhausting. In a sense, the capitalist's fear is well placed, since while the early phases of new technology create tremendous profits, ultimately the following law reasserts itself: that 'surplus-value does not arise from the labour-power that has been replaced by the machinery, but from the labour-power actually employed in working with the machinery' (530). Since surplus-value can only be provided by the presence of humans, not their absence, any emphasis on machinery will ultimately be counterproductive, since, while machines can create the conditions of surplus-value, the apparatus will not in itself produce surplus-value. By replacing workers with machines, the capitalist thus removes the actual source of surplus-value. There is a paradox here. How can machinery both increase and lower the rate of surplus-value?

Section 4. The Factory

The solution to this paradox lies within the factory. Marx begins his discussion, as usual, by specifying his understanding of the term 'factory'. One definition of the factory describes it as the combination of the labour of many workers, another characterizes its workers as subordinated to a vast automaton, a 'self-regulating moving force' (544). Marx claims that while the former emphasizes human control, it is applicable to any use of machinery on a large scale. The latter description is 'characteristic of its use by capital and therefore of the modern factory system'. It is noteworthy that Marx chooses the definition that emphasizes how capitalism disempowers humans as an indirect way of suggesting that there could be a progressive, empowering factory that combines the work of many. Marx tends to present capitalism's negative features not as a result of new technology or modes of production, but as caused by the capitalist desire for profit.

Using his preferred definition, Marx says that in factories, both the tools of workers and their skills are given over to the machine. This increasing reliance on machinery ultimately makes all the factory's workers equal, since it erases the hierarchies of skilled and unskilled labour that we saw emphasized in the Age of Manufacture. The new division of labour in the factory becomes the one between those workers who actually *use* the machines and those that mainly *watch* their operation, with the latter almost always being children. Strangely, if there is any skills advantage in the factory, Marx indicates that it will tend to belong to younger workers, who learn to adapt to new technologies more quickly than older labourers, so that their training periods can be shortened and the experience of older workers can be made to seem useless. There is also a smaller group of a 'superior class of workers', such as engineers and mechanics, but Marx does not consider them crucial to his argument, since the size of this group is small.

If specialized workers in the Age of Manufacture spent their lives handling one tool, industrial workers in a factory spend theirs 'serving the same machine' (547), an obedience that makes the worker's dependence on the factory seem like a modern form of serfdom. Even while supervising a machine may not be physically demanding, it is exhausting anyway, due to the tedium. As it 'deprives the work of all content', the boredom of this kind of work makes workers listless, even as their nerves are shattered by the swift pace of factory production.

Workers now face their 'master', the employer, as someone who has behind him the power of machinery, which delivers 'the face of science, the gigantic natural forces, and the mass of social labour embodied in the system of machinery' (549) to the capitalist. The working individual feels both small and crushed by the superior forces of technology, the electrical and material power of the factory, and the depersonalizing, large numbers of workers in the factory. With these forces, the employer constantly reminds workers that they are merely 'hands' since 'theirs is really a low species of skilled labour' (549). This threat allows for a military-like discipline over workers, whereby the boss can act like his own legislator by instilling a set of 'fines and deductions from wages' (550) for violating his rules. Given the physical danger of factory life and the increasing confinement, Marx says, 'Was Fourier wrong when he called factories "mitigated jails"?' (553).

Section 5. The Struggle Between Worker and Machine

Despite the labourer's domination by the industrial capitalist, Marx considers the factory as a site of working-class struggle. The class struggle 'starts with the existence of the capital-relation itself' (553) and it runs throughout the period of manufacture. Yet only with the onset of machines 'has the worker fought against the instrument of labour itself, capital's material mode of existence' (554). One of these anti-technology attacks came from the early-nineteenth-century Luddites, who destroyed the new machines that put people out of work or allowed their wages to be lowered. Marx understands labourers' anger at the introduction of new equipment, especially as new technology is often used to break strikes and workers' sense of self-determination, but he feels that small-scale acts of defiance, like that of the Luddites, only end by giving the state a 'pretext for the most violent and reactionary measures. It took both time and experience before the workers learnt to distinguish between machinery and its employment by capital, and therefore to transfer their attacks from the material instrument of production to the form of society which utilizes those instruments' (555). The problem lies in the social structure of capitalism, not its instruments. The point is not to condemn invention, but to resist the way it is used to create profit.

Marx also believes that labourers erred in not resisting capitalism at an earlier point, when it was less entrenched. Now when workers resist, they often do so less to overthrow capitalism than to soften its hardest edges. For instance, the struggles 'over wages within the manufacturing system presuppose manufacture, and are in no sense directed against its existence' (555). Rather than workers leading the charge, the initial opposition to the advent of manufactories came instead from the old elites, like the guild masters, who feared being displaced and pushed down to the level of their apprentices. Labourers did not initially oppose the manufactories because these institutions looked to employ landless workers, who desperately needed to exchange their labour-power for wages, in order to purchase the goods and housing needed for survival. Given that the first anticapital-ist-inspired violence came from the yeoman farmers and rural labourers who were driven from the lands, the initial class struggles were between large and (increasingly dispossessed) small farmers, rather than between industrial capital and an urbanized proletariat. At that time, emerging capitalists wanted to make commodities that could be exchanged in the new colonial markets. These manufacturers needed workers to make these commodities and actively looked to employ the rural workers, who had been removed from the feudal social system of agricultural labour largely because of 'very extensive thefts of land' (557), a topic that Marx returns to in Part Eight.

If the manufactories opened their doors to employing labourers, the resulting effect of the division of labour in machinery is entirely the opposite. Industrialists want to remove workers from the factory to save on labour costs. With the arrival of machinery, fewer workers are needed and many can be made unemployed. The ever increasing number of recently sacked workers 'swamps the labour-market' and makes 'the price of labour-power fall below its value' (558), as workers compete with one another for jobs by agreeing to work for less than others. Hence, while machinery cannot directly produce surplus-value, it can do so indirectly by helping capitalists force down wages. As workers demand less money for the same amount of labour-power, the amount of surplus-value increases.

The disempowerment of workers by machinery results initially from the replacement of skilled labourers by low-paid minders of equipment.

Whenever a process requires peculiar dexterity and steadiness of hand, it is withdrawn, as soon as possible, from the cunning workman, who is prone to irregu-larities of many kinds, and it is placed in charge of a peculiar mechanism, so self-regulating that a child can superintend it. (559)

The real impact of machinery is not just that it can

> act as a superior competitor to the worker, always on
> the point of making him superfluous . . . it is the most
> powerful weapon for suppressing strikes, those periodic
> revolts of the working class against the autocracy of
> capital. . . . It would be possible to write a whole history
> of the inventions made since 1830 for the sole purpose
> of providing capital with weapons against working-class
> revolt. (562–3)

Technology is used to teach docility to workers who fear
creating any reason to be fired.

*Section 6. The Compensation Theory, with Regard to the
Workers Displaced by Machinery*

Marx rejects the notion that workers who are made
unemployed in one field, because its processes have been
made more efficient by the introduction of machinery, will
be 'compensated' by getting jobs in the attendant industries
that emerge as a result of the new technologies. To give
a more contemporary example, it is often claimed that if
skilled, manual-labour workers lose their jobs due to the
arrival of computers, then they will get employed by the
companies running the computers or as service sector
workers for the new corporate classes. But Marx says that
'the real facts' (567), as opposed to the fictions of free market
philosophers, are that when workers lose their jobs, they
typically have to look in newer industries that are less
secure, thus creating the possibility of another round of
unemployment, but that such jobs also usually require less
skill and therefore pay less money than their prior ones did.

Jobs may be created when economies are revolutionized, but these are not necessarily jobs that pay well or have the same security.

Marx also indicates that the two industries that are likely to grow in the wake of the technological renovation of industry are the ones that satisfy the 'new luxury requirements' for the new wealth, what we might now call the service sector, and infrastructure, often involving transport and communication industries, that 'can only bear fruit in the distant future, such as the construction of canals, docks, tunnels, bridges and so on. . . . The chief industries of this kind are, at present, gas-works, telegraphy, photography, steam navigation and railways' (573). The service sector in particular increases the number of 'unproductive' workers, not in the sense that they do not work, but that their work does not always produce surplus-value. This category would include servants and members of 'the "ideological" groups, such as members of the government, priests, lawyers, soldiers, etc.', landlords, bankers, and 'paupers, vagabonds and criminals' (574). Workers in transport and communication industries work to prepare for the next round of capitalist advances based on a reduction of lost time, but Marx defers a longer discussion of the relationship between production and circulation industries to later volumes of *Capital*.

Section 7. Repulsion and Attraction of Workers Through the Development of Machine Production. Crises in the Cotton Industry

Just as large-scale industries push workers from one workplace to another, machinery sets off a domino-like effect of new technologies through industries. Capitalist development keeps accelerating as large-scale industry has the 'capacity of sudden extension by leaps and bounds' and new technology opens up the demand for more raw materials that can be processed into commodities: 'the invention of the cotton gin increased the production of cotton' (579). This surge undermines those other capitalists who lack the advantage of recent technological advances:

> As long as machine production expands in a given branch of industry at the expense of the old handicrafts or of manufacture, the result is as certain as is the result of an encounter between an army with breach-loading rifles and one with bows and arrows. (578)

> [T]he cheapness of the articles produced by machinery and the revolution in the means of transport and communication provide the weapons for the conquest of foreign markets. By ruining handicraft production of finished articles in other countries, machinery forcibly converts them into fields for the production of its raw material. Thus India was compelled to produce cotton, wool, hemp, jute and indigo for Great Britain. (579)

Capitalists begin to create a 'new and international division of labour' (579) as the colonies' older industries are smashed and the region is turned to the production of raw materials, a move that 'converts one part of the globe into a chiefly agricultural field of production for supplying the other part, which remains a pre-eminently industrial field' (580). In a larger sense, capitalism in one nation tries to prevent other countries from being its equals or competitors.

Yet large-scale industry's ability to produce so many more commodities than in the past throws capitalists into recurring crises of overproduction.

> The factory system's tremendous capacity for expanding with sudden immense leaps, and its dependence on the world market, necessarily give rise to the following cycle: feverish production, a consequent glut on the market, then a contraction of the market which causes production to be crippled. The life of industry becomes a series of periods of moderate activity, prosperity, over-production, crisis and stagnation. (580)

The effect of this cycle is that labourers are 'continually repelled and attracted, slung backwards and forwards, while, at the same time, constant changes take place in the sex, age and skill of the industrial conscripts' (583) as capitalists use different components of the workforce against one another. The chaos of capitalist expansion and retraction causes tremendous damage to workers who must live with the uncertainty of cyclical hirings and firings. Marx concludes this section by documenting the cyclical history of industrial employment in England, while also showing how these recurring crises of overproduction have negative global effects for all the regions connected to England via the world market.

Section 8. The Revolutionary Impact of Large-Scale Industry on Manufacture, Handicrafts and Domestic Industry

Machinery's creation of unskilled labour is accompanied by the dreadful housing and the environmental, health, and cultural damage that industrial capital produces in the wake of the prior age's co-operation and division of labour. This section's account of the deplorable conditions of the English labouring class makes gripping reading. Marx also emphasizes that revolutions in transport and information flow destroy the older 'seasons' of more and then less intensive labour, because of the globalized market's never-ending demand for goods. As capitalists seek to reduce the time required by a cycle of trade, the cycles of production and consumption become shorter in ways that both erase the old time patterns and create a new sense of time, a capitalist temporality, that increasingly involves working around the clock.

Section 9. The Health and Education Clauses of the Factory Acts. The General Extension of Factory Legislation in England

The horrors of machinery include industrial accidents that maim and kill workers. One counterbalance was the passage of laws designed to protect workers. Marx shows, however, that industrial capitalists usually evade the obligations placed on them by even the slightest of legislation with regard to the health and welfare of workers. Indeed, capitalism does not want to make labourers more secure; it wants to structure insecurity in the lives of the proletariat. The key means of doing so involve the creation of 'that monstrosity, the disposable working population held in reserve' (618). This is the group of the unemployed that is held 'in misery, for the changing requirements of capitalist exploitation' (618).

Before turning to discuss the creation of unemployment, Marx underlines how capitalism always searches for the weak or vulnerable to exploit and works to undermine any social space that might resist it. Whenever 'capital is subjected to state control, even at the handful of points on the periphery of society, it seeks compensation all the more unrestrainedly at all other points' (621). Capitalists resist labour laws, attack unions, and destroy the old trades as ways of life that were 'previously a safety-valve for the whole social mechanism' (635) as they provide sanctuary from capitalist practices. To this end, capitalists also revolutionize agriculture in order to dismantle the peasantry. Consequently 'the need for social transformation, and the antagonism of the classes, reaches the same level in the countryside as it has attained in the towns' (637). We often think of capitalism as purely an urban phenomenon, but Marx consistently argues that capitalist practices wreak their first damage on rural labourers. As capitalism 'disturbs the metabolic interaction between man and earth', disposed backcountry farmers swirl into the slums of the cities in ways that damage 'at the same time the physical health of the urban worker, and the intellectual life of the rural worker' (638).

Yet while the first effects of capitalism's commodification of labour are borne by those outside of the cities, the first awareness of a proletarian identity takes root in the cities. As the 'dispersal of the rural workers over large areas breaks their power of resistance', their concentration within the cities 'increases that of the urban worker' (638), perhaps because the anger of the newly dispossessed revitalizes those who have become passive and resigned to the new order. In like fashion, some aspects of capitalism's destruction of older social systems are positive. For instance, the introduction of female and younger workers in the factory partially frees them from an infantilizing imprisonment by husbands and fathers. By making women more independent, capitalism creates a

> new economic foundation for a higher form of the family and of relations between the sexes. It is of course just as absurd to regard the Christian–Germanic form of the family as absolute and final as it would have been in the case of the ancient Roman, the ancient Greek or the Oriental forms, which, moreover, form a series in historical development. (621)

Capitalists' creation of a 'collective working group' composed of both genders and all ages can be used as a progressive model for 'human development' and more egalitarian relations in a post-capitalist society.

Part Five: The Production of Absolute and Relative Surplus-Value

Chapter 16. Absolute and Relative Surplus-Value

In this transitional part, Marx reiterates some of his previous points and definitions. A 'productive worker' is

> one who produces surplus-value for the capitalist or in other words contributes towards the self-valorization of capital. If we may take an example from outside the sphere of material production, a schoolmaster is a productive worker when, in addition to belabouring the heads of his pupils, he works himself into the ground to enrich the owner of the school. That the latter has laid out his capital in a teaching factory, instead of a sausage factory, makes no difference to the relation . . . to be a productive worker is therefore not a piece of luck, but a misfortune. (644)

A teacher or artist might make use-values for her or his audience, but becomes 'productive' only when these use-values are marketed with an eye to profit.

Arguing that the capital-relation comes out of a 'long process of development' that unfolded over centuries, Marx suggests that it arises first in nations in the 'temperate zone', since those in warmer climes have had nature provide goods for them. If ancient cultures, like Egypt, undertook 'gigantic building projects', this was because they had large populations with freely disposable labour, which had to be kept busy in case they revolted. Capitalist societies differ from ancient societies, as we shall see, because capitalism wants a surplus population to remain without work.

Chapter 17. Changes of Magnitude in the Price of Labour-Power and in Surplus-Value

Chapter 18. Different Formulae for the Rate of Surplus-value

In these chapters, Marx shows that the 'relative magnitudes of surplus-value and of price of labour-power' (655) have three determinants: the length of the working day (the extensive magnitude of labour); the intensity of labour (the intensive magnitude of labour); and the productivity of labour. These three elements are somewhat independent of each other, as one might increase without changing the size of surplus-value if the other two provide counterweights. Chapter 18 goes through different complex formulae to end by insisting that capital

is not only the command over labour, as Adam Smith thought. It is essentially the command over unpaid labour. . . . The secret of the self-valorization of capital resolves itself into the fact that it has at its disposal a definite quantity of the unpaid labour of other people. (672)

Part Six: Wages

Chapter 19. The Transformation of the Value
(and Respectively the Price) of Labour-Power into Wages

Chapter 20. Time-Wages

Chapter 21. Piece-Wages

Chapter 22. National Differences in Wages

This part repeats the claim that the magnitude of surplus-value is determined by the length of the working day (absolute surplus-value), the intensity of labour, and the productivity of labour (these last two combine the features of relative surplus-value: co-operation, specialized labour, and machinery).

There remains one other aspect that affects the magnitude of surplus-value and that is the wages that labourers are paid. Wages are the intermediary money-form that prices the value of the worker's labour-power. Marx reminds us that it is not labour that is traded, but labour-power; labour-power is labour that has been turned into a commodity, something that is quantified to be exchanged; 'labour is the substance and the immanent measure of value, but it has no value itself' (677), it has to be sold in a 'transformed condition as wages'.

Marx repeats these points in order to disagree with Adam Smith, who argues that the price of a commodity is determined by its supply and demand. Marx argues that this claim can only be held if we follow Smith in assuming that the supply of labour is a natural element, which is not politically and historically transformable. In one sense, the remaining parts of *Capital* are intended to disprove Smith's claim, since Marx will argue that capitalists actively change the supply and demand of labour by using machinery to create a new supply of workers willing to work for lower wages. Analysing the market in terms of supply and demand only makes 'the actual relation [between capitalist and labourer] invisible, and indeed presents to the eye the precise opposite of that relation' (680). The idea of supply and demand is like the commodity fetish that seems true only because we have not fully exposed its material context.

For example, it is not the supply and demand of commodities that causes prices to rise, but the supply and demand of the labour-power that makes commodities. When the cost of purchasing labour-power increases, so, too, do the prices of the goods that a labourer makes. One way to safeguard the level of surplus-value is to pay labourers their wages at an hourly rate rather than as a lump monthly or yearly sum. This masks capitalists' ability to prolong the working day by the pretence of 'overtime'. While workers are often paid better for their overtime, Marx argues that this increase is often 'ridiculously small' (687) and is counterbalanced by the freedom capitalists have to reduce waged work when labour is not needed.

An even more effective method capitalists employ to gain surplus-value is to pay labourers by the number of objects they make, in what is called 'the sweating system' (we often call textile shops that use this system 'sweatshops'). This system of payment is highly profitable for the employer, since he or she is essentially paying only for the employee's work, not for their time breaks. It also helps to intensify labour, as workers continually push themselves to make more objects. Piece-wages thus become 'the most fruitful source of reductions in wages, and of frauds committed by the capitalists' (694).

Historically, sweatshops in the West were mainly run using the labour of ethnic immigrants, primarily women. Today, sweated labour often occurs in non-Western lands, the so-called developing economic regions, where local populations function like immigrants as they work in foreign controlled factory zones and receive pitifully small piece-wages to produce clothing for Western consumers.

Marx ends this part by noting that every nation has its own average levels of labour, and that wage levels differ in different countries, depending on their productivity.

Part Seven: The Process of Accumulation of Capital

In the brief prologue to Part Seven, Marx foreshadows two arguments that he will later take up in the second and third volumes of *Capital*. The second volume examines the movement of value through the spheres of circulation and production, and the third looks at how a capitalist has to share the profit with other capitalists 'who fulfil other functions in social production taken as a whole' (709) – for instance, with the owners of land that he rents. These two relationships are too complex for Marx's purpose here, and he continues to focus on his basic outline in this volume. Marx briefly mentions these aspects to indicate that he is aware of the complex factors involved, but that he wants to present the fundamentals before moving on to even more technical matters.

Chapter 23. Simple Reproduction

In the first two parts, Marx clarifies the nature of value, which can admittedly be a difficult concept to grasp. In the middle parts, he provides a concrete historical account that illustrates how the search for surplus-value sets into motion a series of class struggles that last for centuries. In the last parts of the volume, Marx combines these two aspects:

he returns to describing the general aspects of capital as a phenomenon that lasts over several generations and then moves on to his long delayed discussion of the early events that catalysed the possibility for capitalist profiteering.

In this chapter, Marx introduces the question of simple reproduction. Initially capital was spent to produce a commodity to be sold for more surplus-value. Yet since each society's conditions of production are simultaneously the conditions for renewing itself, we should not only consider capital as a matter of production, but also as one of re-production, a circuit of repeatable productions.

> Whatever the social form of the production process, it has to be continuous, it must periodically repeat the same phases . . . and in the constant flux of its incessant renewal, every social process of production is at the same time a process of reproduction. (711)

Until now Marx's argument has only assumed a simple cycle of trades, where the capitalist did not have to concern himself with the 'maintenance and reproduction of the working class' (718) in terms of what labourers do outside of the workspace. This limited viewpoint is not strictly true, since capitalist production must perpetuate 'the conditions under which the worker is exploited' (723). If labourers produce surplus-value, capitalists must reproduce class relations or the 'capital-relation itself: on the one hand the capitalist; on the other the wage-labourer', (724) who must commodify himself. The reproduction of the working class is a prerequisite for the reproduction of capital.

The exchange of labour-power for wages usually occurs through the 'legal fiction of a contract' (719), enforced by law, which seems as if it exists only for a single exchange. Despite the momentary appearance of the work contract, formed only in the moment of mutual consent between buyer and seller, 'in reality the worker belongs to capital before he has sold himself to the capitalist. His economic bondage' comes from the life conditions that workers exist in before any specific work agreement has been made (723). Labourers are at a structural disadvantage even before they meet the buyers of their labour-power. Because they come seeking to sell their labour-power to satisfy pressing basic needs, they have little room for manoeuvre to escape from the unfair wage contracts offered to them.

Chapter 24. The Transformation of Surplus-Value into Capital

Section 1. Capitalist Production on a Progressively Increasing Scale. The Inversion Which Converts the Property Laws of Commodity Production into Laws of Capitalist Appropriation

When considering the reproduction of capitalist relations, recall that while capital creates surplus-value, 'the employment of surplus-value as capital, or its reconversion into capital, is called accumulation of capital' (725). Keep in mind that capital is surplus-value that is used to create more surplus-value (or to go back to the earlier formula, money that buys commodities to sell them for money and profit: M–C–(M + ΔM)). As surplus-value looks to make more surplus-value, capital's repetition exists in an expanding feedback loop that is more like a spiral, where each turn generates an increasing domain, rather than a simple circle.

The simple reproduction of capital can be explained by the basic elements that happen as money is transformed into capital: the end product belongs to the capitalist, not the worker; the product was made by consuming the worker's labour-power, which produces a surplus-value 'which costs the worker labour but the capitalist nothing', and, at the end, the capitalist has the commodity while the labourer must sell his or her labour again. 'Simple reproduction is only the periodic repetition of this first step' (731).

Yet after the first cycle is completed, the process begins all over again. This happens firstly because the worker still needs to eat and survive and must therefore go back and sell her or his labour. Secondly, the capitalist has surplus-value, which must be reinvested, since its main purpose is to create exchange-value, not use-value.

Section 2. The Political Economists' Erroneous Conception of Reproduction on an Increasing Scale

Section 3. Division of Surplus-Value into Capital and Revenue. The Abstinence Theory

Section 4. The Circumstances Which, Independently of the Proportional Division of Surplus-Value into Capital and Revenue, Determine the Extent of Accumulation, Namely, the Degree of Exploitation of Labour-Power, the Productivity of Labour, the Growing Difference in Amount Between Capital Employed and Capital Consumed, and the Magnitude of the Capital Advanced

In these sections, Marx responds again to errors in the writings of classical political economy that take the capitalist market as their norm. These economists want to defend bourgeois capitalism by contrasting it with the spectacular consumption and taste for luxury of the aristocracy, and consequently they argue that, in capitalism, all surplus value is reused to buy new variable capital (more labour-power). Marx argues that this is strictly not the case, as some of the surplus also goes back into constant capital: machinery must be replaced due to wear and tear, and raw materials need to be replenished.

There is also a tension within each capitalist regarding whether he should consume his surplus-value by buying luxuries to reward himself or show 'abstinence' by reinvesting capital for 'progressive accumulation' (739), or 'accumulation for the sake of accumulation, production for the sake of production' (742). The conflict 'between the passion for accumulation and the desire for enjoyment' (741) beats on in the capitalist's heart, and Marx notes the tendency in later generations of capitalists to spend more on luxuries. Yet if anyone's consumer desires are to be policed, they will not be those of the capitalist class, but those of the working class, since if they can be taught to 'desire' less food and other commodities, then the size of their necessary labour reduces, thus giving the capitalist more surplus-value. If labourers refuse to limit their consumption, then capitalists will increase surplus-value by seizing more land and human labour-power as the 'two primary creators of wealth' (752). This theme of theft preoccupies Marx for the remainder of the volume.

Section 5. The So-Called Labour Fund

Continuing from the previous chapter, Marx reinstates that 'capital is not a fixed magnitude, but a part of social wealth, which is elastic and constantly fluctuates with the division of surplus-value into revenue and additional capital' (768). Land, labour-power, and science (new inventions) all give capital the power to expand. This is particularly true with variable capital, since the amount of labour-power available for exploitation is not a fixed, naturally appearing amount, but one socially constructed by capitalists. The classical economists, such as the utilitarians Jeremy Bentham, John Stuart Mill, and Thomas Malthus, talked about a 'labour-fund' as if it were like a natural resource. 'But the number of workers . . . is not given, for it changes with the degree of exploitation of the individual labour-power' (759–60). Similarly, wage prices can also change. To show that classical economists' complacency about the presence of the working class is mistaken, Marx turns, in the next chapter, to documenting the General Law of Capitalist Accumulation. Recall that Chapter 4 defined the General Law for Capital as the production of surplus-value. The General Law of Capitalist Accumulation focuses not on the production of surplus, but on the reproduction of the class relations that generate surplus. What we initially learned conceptually will now be explained through material relations.

Chapter 25. The General Law of Capitalist Accumulation

Section 1. A Growing Demand for Labour-Power Accompanies Accumulation if the Composition of Capital Remains the Same

Before considering the 'influence of the growth of capital on the fate of the working-class' (762), Marx presents a series of somewhat complicated terms involving capital. The important term, though, is the *organic composition* of capital, defined as the ratio between the mass of the means of production employed (constant capital) and the mass of labour necessary for its employment (variable capital). For capital to grow, it must increase the size of labour-power in relation to constant capital. Yet if the current supply of workers' labour-power is not enough for the capitalists' collective needs, then labourers will use the scarcity to demand higher wages, as was especially the case in the fifteenth century and in the first half of the eighteenth century. If capital continually grows, then 'sooner or later a point must be reached at which the requirements of accumulation begin to outgrow the customary supply of labour, and a rise of wages therefore takes place' (763). To lower their wage costs, capitalists need the pressure of unemployed workers, who will increase the competition among workers by offering to work for lower wages. 'Accumulation of capital is therefore multiplication of the proletariat' (764). The definition of a proletarian is 'nothing other than "wage-labourer", the man who produces and valorizes "capital", and is thrown onto the street as soon as he becomes superfluous to the need for valorization possessed by "Monsieur Capital"' (764).

Given that 'the production of surplus-value or making of profits is the absolute law of this [capitalist] mode of production' (769) and that surplus-value comes from unpaid labour, we can consider the production of surplus-value both in terms of a *mode of production* and what we might call a *mode of reproduction*. Marx has treated the former in his discussion of absolute and relative surplus-value. The latter involves a consideration of the social pressures on and within the working class. At the end of a business cycle, the capitalist has the money that he used to purchase labour-power along with the surplus of profit. After subtracting his own use needs, the capitalist then reinvests the original money and its profit. Since the commodity that the capitalist buys is labour-power, the profit from the first cycle will need to buy more labour-power, hence more labourers.

According to the theory of supply and demand, when the supply of labourers decreases (since capitalists look to buy up all the labour-power they can find), workers will use the increased demand for their labour-power to bargain for higher wages. And, of course, this happens. Marx counters, though, by arguing that capital responds to wage pressures by using increased efficiency of the production process to reduce the number of workers needed. The 'relation between the unpaid labour transformed into capital' (surplus labour) and 'the additional paid labour necessary to set in motion this additional capital' (necessary labour) involves 'the relation between the unpaid and paid labour of the same working population' (771). The reproduction of capital is thus the transformation of labourers into paid, employed proletarians as well as unpaid, unemployed proletarians, whose desire for work at any wage will give the capitalist a tool to lower the wages of those actually working.

Section 2. A Relative Diminution of the Variable Part of Capital Occurs in the Course of the Further Progress of Accumulation and of the Concentration Accompanying It

While capitalists create unemployment to pit workers against each other, they effectively do the same with each other. Capitalists will tend to concentrate industries by creating centralized monopolies that push smaller capitalists under. Marx indicates that he will not develop the theme of 'the attraction of capital by capital' (777), but

How to Read Marx's *Capital*

says that the 'transformation of many small into few large capitals' (777) is 'fought by the cheapening of commodities', where the 'two most powerful levers of centralization' are 'competition and credit' (779). The centralization of capital usually involves one figure (or corporate entity) extending the scale of his operation, usually through the 'violent method of annexation' or through the use of 'joint-stock companies' to raise credit (779). As fewer capitalists emerge in the wake of competition, the dominant players are able to become even more dominant by using credit to invest in new machinery; this makes their commodities cheaper and drives competitors into financial ruin as they are forced to match the new lower prices even though their capital costs have not decreased, and so they lose profit. Marx differentiates the mere concentration of resources from what he calls centralization, increasing ownership by fewer individuals, as centralization greatly accelerates what had previously been a 'gradual increase of capital'.

Section 3. The Progressive Production of a Relative Surplus Population or Industrial Reserve Army

Here Marx finally blows up the theory of supply and demand as he shows that supply is a socially manipulated phenomenon, in which the upper hand lies with the capitalists (in the same way that the work contract only looks equal, but in fact depends on a false freedom for the labourers, who must sell their labour-power). The initial effect of 'increasing accumulation and centralization' of capital is the change in the organic composition as capitalists increasingly rely on constant capital (machinery) rather than variable capital (labour-power). There is a paradox and a solution in the increasing reliance on machinery. On the one hand, machinery is attractive because it allows for commodities to be made more cheaply because fewer workers are necessary to produce them. On the other hand, the reduction of variable capital also reduces the rate of surplus-value, since only humans can create value. Thus, the reliance on machinery initially benefits capitalists, while also damaging them. This contradiction is resolved as technology's implementation increases unemployment, so that capitalists can regenerate surplus-value by using the fear of unemployment to depress workers' wages, resulting in labourers giving over more surplus-value to the owners.

> But if a surplus population of workers is a necessary product of accumulation or of the development of wealth on a capitalist basis, this surplus population also becomes, conversely, the lever of capitalist accumulation, indeed it becomes a condition for the existence of the capitalist mode of production. It forms a disposable industrial reserve army, which belongs to capital just as absolutely as if the latter had bred it at its own cost. (784)

The influential political economist Thomas Malthus, using a simple model of supply and demand, argues that population naturally and absolutely increases as humans reproduce until the scarcity of natural resources threatens the survival of the existing population. Marx, conversely, suggests that while this may be true in non-capitalist societies, in capitalist ones a 'surplus population' of labourers is created beyond their possible employment because it is the 'condition for the existence of capital', even, and we might say especially, if the increased population pushes labourers into lives of misery and want. It is the presence of this relative surplus population that ensures the reproduction of class relations and the desperation of workers on which capitalism depends to generate surplus-value. No capitalist society will ever reduce unemployment because joblessness is the plank upon which it rests. Conversely, a 'Welfare State' that promises full employment or unemployment benefits (and housing) will always be a target of hostility by business interests.

Section 4. Different Forms of Existence of the Relative Surplus Population. The General Law of Capitalist Accumulation

There are three forms of relative surplus population: floating, latent, and stagnant. The floating form involves the urbanized working population that is irregularly employed. Sometimes workers emigrate to follow capital in search of jobs – they 'float' to be employed. The latent surplus population consists of labourers who have come from the countryside, no matter how broadly defined, who have not yet become proletarians, but might become so. Marx calls this labour 'latent' because it can be called upon to work when necessary. Those included in the category of 'stagnant' are people with 'extremely irregular employment', casualized labourers who are willing to take very low wages for jobs with short contracts and little security or benefits (796). Below even these labourers is the 'lowest sediment' that 'dwells in pauperism. Apart from vagabonds, criminals, prostitutes [what Marx calls the "lumpenproletariat"] . . . this social stratum consists of three categories' (797): (1) those who are able to work but have been thrown into extreme poverty; (2) orphans and pauper children; and (3) the demoralized, the ragged, and those unable to work, chiefly people who succumb to their incapacity for adaptation, an incapacity which results from the division of labour; people who have lived beyond the worker's average life-span; and the victims of industry . . . the mutilated, the sickly, the widows, etc.

These people decrease the earnings of labourers not because they compete with them for jobs, but because the costs of caring for them are typically borne by the working class. 'Pauperism is the hospital of the active labour-army and the dead weight of the industrial reserve army . . . [since] capital usually knows how to transfer these from its own shoulders to those of the working class and the petty bourgeoisie' (797).

Marx now comes to the point that he has been leading to when he declares that the increase of capital creates a decrease in the life conditions of workers through the technique of structured unemployment.

The greater the social wealth, the functioning capital, the extent and energy of its growth, and therefore also the greater the absolute mass of the proletariat and the productivity of its labour, the greater is the industrial reserve army. The same causes which develop the expansive power of capital, also develop the labour-power at its disposal . . . the more extensive, finally, the pauperized sections of the working class and the industrial reserve army, the greater is the official pauperism. *This is the absolute general law of capitalist accumulation.* (798)

Capital produces working-class misery:

> In proportion as capital accumulates, the situation of the worker, be his payment high or low, must grow worse. . . . Accumulation of wealth at one pole is, therefore, at the same time accumulation of misery, the torment of labour, slavery, ignorance, brutalization and moral degradation at the opposite pole, i.e. on the side of the class that produces its own product as capital. (799)

Capital structurally, not accidentally, produces human wretchedness and anxiety, and this misery continues to expand and accumulate because capitalism is a system that must itself expand in order to accumulate (surplus-value must be reinvested to gain more surplus-value).

Having shown that capitalism will always generate a surplus of labour to satisfy its demand, Marx asks the question: How did capitalists get an amount of surplus-value, in the first place, to invest as capital? How did capitalism begin? If one needs capital to make capital, where did anyone get the original capital (primary accumulation)? This riddle of capitalism's origin is the theme of *Capital*'s final part.

Section 5: Illustrations of the Law of Capitalist Accumulation

Before answering how capitalism begins, Marx again takes time to provide harrowing details about the law of capitalist accumulation by reviewing the terrible working and housing conditions throughout the rise of industrialized England during the nineteenth century. Marx devotes numerous pages to reciting official statistics about urban overcrowding, disease, mortality, and the plight of the rural wandering population living in what we might consider mobile slums without sanitation. Given the capitalist appropriation of agriculture, this misery takes place as much in the countryside as it does in the city. He recites a county-by-county list to show that the capitalist reconfiguration of farming has created overcrowding and deprivation in the countryside as well, which is no pastoral place of escape for the working class. Lastly, the same is true in the colonies, represented here by Ireland, where even mass emigration to America cannot uplift its terrible conditions. Global capitalism is global misery.

Part Eight: So-Called Primitive ['Originating'] Accumulation

Chapter 26. The Secret of Primitive Accumulation

Capital begins with one secret, the secret of commodity fetishism, and ends with another, the secret of so-called primitive accumulation. Despite lengthy treatments about how capitalism works, Marx has not explained how the capitalist system *began*. There's a sort of chicken-and-egg riddle regarding capital, given that 'the accumulation of capital presupposes surplus-value' and 'surplus-value presupposes capitalist production' (873). How can we get out of this contradiction? Liberal political economy has its answer with a fable about something like original sin: 'Long, long ago there were two sorts of people; one, the diligent, intelligent and above all frugal elite; the other, lazy rascals, spending their substance, and more, in riotous living' (873). The class system emerged from these two mentalities, as 'it came to pass that the former sort accumulated wealth, and the latter sort finally had nothing to sell except their own skins'. Marx thinks that the notion that some people worked harder than others to become wealthy is childish. Instead, he believes the initial source of capital to be violence. 'In actual history, it is a notorious fact that conquest, enslavement, robbery, murder, in short, force, play the greatest part. . . .

[T]he methods of primitive accumulation were anything but idyllic' (874).

The violence that originates capitalism arises because it requires 'free workers' in the double sense of workers who 'neither form part of the means of production themselves, as would be the case with slaves, serfs, etc., nor do they own the means of production'. Capitalist production not only depends on this separation but 'reproduces it on a constantly extending scale. The process, therefore, which creates the capital-relation can be nothing other than the process which divorces the worker from the ownership of the conditions of his own labour' (874). This is the process by which

> the social means of subsistence and production are turned into capital, and the immediate producers are turned into wage-labourers. So-called primitive accumulation, therefore, is nothing else than the historical process of divorcing the producer from the means of production. It appears as 'primitive' because it forms the prehistory of capital, and of the mode of production corresponding to capital. (875)

With the phrase 'primitive accumulation', we have another example of how English translations can obscure Marx's meaning. Marx's *ursprüngliche Akkumulation* is better understood as 'originating accumulation', in the sense of the first accumulation that is turned into capital, rather than 'primitive accumulation', which to contemporary ears has the connotation of non-European or prehistoric activity. 'Originating' also carries the notion that every new cycle of capitalism resorts to violence. The reproduction of capital is the regeneration of violence.

Capitalism emerges from the European feudal social system as it wrenches subjects from either the land or the restrictive labour practices of the guilds. The emerging capitalism had to confront both feudalism and the guilds, but it did so by benefiting from events that it did not create. A starting point glimmers with the 'first sporadic traces of capitalist production as early as the fourteenth or fifteenth centuries in certain towns of the Mediterranean', such as Florence, Venice, and Genoa, but 'the capitalist era dates from the sixteenth century' (876). By the time that capitalism appears as a stable phenomenon, serfdom has already been abolished and the 'independent city-states' of the Middle Ages, which were the guilds' strongholds, were on the wane. As workers experienced 'emancipation from serfdom and the fetters of the guilds' (875), they became 'free' to sell their labour-power.

Marx now uses the history of England as his case study for the separation of farmers from their land, as 'great masses of men are suddenly and forcibly turned from their means of subsistence, and hurled into the labour-market as free, unprotected and rightless proletarians' (876). Although Marx chooses his examples from England, he also notes that similar processes exist elsewhere, albeit with local variations.

The history of this expropriation assumes different aspects in different countries, and runs through its various phases in different orders of succession, and at different historical epochs. Only in England, which we therefore take as our example, has it the classic form. (876)

We might wonder why Marx considers England the 'classic form'. He seems to grant England this status mainly because he considers (industrial) capitalism to be more advanced there than in either France or Germany, the two other strongly capitalist nations. This assumption may or may not be true; but England does provide Marx with something that the continent does not: it is 'the only country to possess a continuous set of official statistics relating to the matters' (349 n.15) that Marx is considering.

Chapter 27. The Expropriation of the Agricultural Population from the Land

The possibility for the historical emergence of capitalist activity begins when the feudal structure of farmers bound to land starts to vanish. 'In England, serfdom had disappeared in practice by the last part of the fourteenth century' (877), especially after the Black Death (mentioned on page 861) caused population decreases that gave the remaining field workers more leverage to demand rights. At this point, the majority of the population were still 'free peasant proprietors' who owned some land, and, more importantly, had rights to 'common land, which gave pasture to their cattle, and furnished them with timber, fire-wood, turf, etc.' The commons was land that was not privately controlled by a single owner, like the local aristocrat. The combination of small freehold farms and access to the commons gave a protective means of production to villagers. In order to create free and unattached proletarians,

the great feudal lords, in their defiant opposition to the king and Parliament, created an incomparably larger proletariat by forcibly driving the peasantry from the land, to which the latter had the same feudal title as the lords themselves, and by usurpation of the common lands. (877)

The chance for this occurs due to 'the rapid expansion of wool manufacture in Flanders and the corresponding rise in the price of wool in England' (878–9). 'The old nobility had been devoured by the great feudal wars. The new nobility was the child of its time, for which money was the power of all powers. Transformation of arable land into sheep-walks was therefore its slogan' (879). During the fifteenth century, the Norman aristocratic order had weakened through civil wars, and an emergent noble class sought to integrate a still relatively isolated England into the European world market by providing raw materials (wool) for the Continental textile manufacturers.

The process that 'precipitated' the English working class from 'its golden age to its iron age' was enclosure, whereby arable farming land was turned into pasture for wool-producing sheep. Communal land was often taken by force from the villagers by the rising aristocracy, who erected fences around the land to prevent the sheep from wandering, destroyed village housing, and sent off its former inhabitants to fend for themselves. While laws were enacted throughout the seventeenth century with the intention of preventing the destruction of small farmers by insisting that any home had land attached to it, the 'process of forcible expropriation' received a new impulse through Henry VIII's dissolution of the Catholic Church.

The estates of the church were to a large extent given away to rapacious royal favourites, or sold at a nominal price to speculating farmers and townsmen, who drove out the old-established hereditary sub-tenants in great numbers, and threw their holdings together. (881–2)

'The legally guaranteed property of the poorer folk' was 'quietly confiscated', the people were pauperized, and the period saw an astonishing increase in poverty. This was due to the rise of a new kind of long-distance, market-oriented farm owner, who removed the feudal customs, which had provided a limited form of protection and had guaranteed the right to use common land.

The 'class of independent peasants' had been the backbone of Cromwell's army, which fought against the gentry, but by 'about 1750 the yeomanry had disappeared' (883). The arrival of William of Orange after the 'glorious Revolution' of 1688 empowered a new group of 'landed and capitalist profit-grubbers', who practised 'on a colossal scale . . . thefts of state lands which had hitherto been managed more modestly' (884). This 'new landed aristocracy' was closely allied to the 'new bankocracy, of newly hatched high finance, and of the large manufacturers, at that time dependent on protective duties' (885). The theft of communal property accelerated in the eighteenth century, because capitalists had for the first time the advantage of the state legislating in their favour with Parliamentary bills: 'the law itself now becomes the instrument by which the people's land is stolen' (885). Now those working the land on the large farms became 'tenants at will, small farmers on yearly leases, a servile rabble dependent on the arbitrary will of the landlords' (886). Directly criticizing Adam Smith,

Marx says, 'The eighteenth century, however, did not yet recognize as fully as the nineteenth the identity between the wealth of the nation and the poverty of the people' (886). Unlike Smith, Marx does not believe that free trade increased wealth in the eighteenth century, but instead, that wealth resulted from a 'whole series of thefts, outrages and popular misery that accompanied the forcible expropriation of the people, from the last third of the fifteenth to the end of the eighteenth century' (889).

> The spoliation of the Church's property, the fraudulent alienation of the state domains, the theft of common lands, the usurpation of feudal and clan property and its transformation into modern private property under circumstances of ruthless terrorism, all these things were just so many idyllic methods of primitive accumulation. They conquered the field for capitalist agriculture, incorporated the soil into capital, and created for the urban industries the necessary supplies of free and rightless proletarians. (895)

This act of appropriation massively increased poverty and 'by the nineteenth century, the very memory of the connection between the agricultural labourer and communal property had, of course, vanished' (889). In Scotland, this occurred partly because the older 'tribal' structure was transformed after it had been superseded by English rule, as many clan chiefs became complicit with capitalist interests, acting as middlemen to control their clanspeople for the restructuring of land ownership. This 'clearing of estates' becomes romanticized in the period's historical fiction, like that of Walter Scott, which provides a fantastically nostalgic and fundamentally false image of the time. After the world market no longer required wool, due to the rise of cotton as a wool substitute, the enclosed lands did not revert back to communal ownership, but were turned into leisure hunting grounds for the wealthy.

Chapter 28. Bloody Legislation Against the Expropriated Since the End of the Fifteenth Century. The Forcing Down of Wages by Act of Parliament

As landless peasants were forced off the lands by the manor's lords, 'they were turned in massive quantities into beggars, robbers and vagabonds, partly from inclination, in most cases under the force of circumstances' (896). Rather than help the impoverished, the monarchy passed a series of ruthless laws that criminalized being homeless and demanded torture-like punishments for being poor. The purpose of this 'bloody legislation' was to force the newly landless into commodifying their labour and passively accepting the new work conditions in the manufactories. 'Thus were the agricultural folk first expropriated from the soil, driven from their homes, turned into vagabonds, and then whipped, branded and tortured by grotesquely terroristic laws into accepting the discipline necessary for the system of wage-labour' (899). The rising bourgeoisie relied on the power of the state to regulate wages and force the labouring class into new, longer, and harder work conditions, producing absolute surplus-value. 'Worker combinations', an early form of unions, were criminalized until 1825, 'in the face of the threatening attitude of the proletariat' (903). At every point, while the bourgeoisie fought for their own freedom, they simultaneously prevented labourers from achieving the same rights. This was also the case during the French Revolution, when Le Chapelier's law declared that every combination by the workers was 'an assault on liberty and the declaration of the rights of man' (903) – in other words, on the freedom of capitalists to exploit labourers.

Chapter 29. The Genesis of the Capitalist Farmer

Having explained the origin of the proletariat, Marx turns to the question, 'Where did capitalists originally spring from?' to answer: 'the great landed proprietors' (905). While we often think of capitalism as beginning in the cities, Marx argues that it first appears in the countryside, during the 'agricultural revolution which began in the last third of the fifteenth century and continued during the bulk of the sixteenth', driven by a newly emerging kind of capitalist farmer (905–6). These farmers gained money because the sixteenth century saw a prolonged period of inflation that lowered the wages they paid their labourers, reduced the annual rents they paid to the manor lords – since these had been fixed in 99-year contracts – and raised the price of the food and field goods that they sold. With lower labour and rent costs, but increased profits, a class of previously 'free small-scale proprietors' became 'capitalist farmers' (905), who benefited from the enclosures to appear as a 'middle class' between the landed gentry and the peasantry.

Chapter 30. Impact of the Agricultural Revolution on Industry. The Creation of a Home Market for Industrial Capital

As a result of capitalist agriculture's turning peasants off the land, formerly rural labourers began to arrive in the cities, looking for work in the manufactories outside of the securities of the guild structure. Marx cautions us though to remember that capitalist-driven changes in the manufacturing period advance in a slow and sporadic fashion, often collapsing in ways that allow for the return of older ways of working. One reason for the period's inconsistencies is that the English manufacturers still had to rely on the countryside to provide raw materials and purchase their goods, and the capitalist revolution in agriculture had not yet entirely destroyed the older rural domestic industry. Only with the onset of large-scale industry were capitalists able to separate agriculture from rural domestic industry and force farmers to purchase goods from factories, rather than the goods that were made regionally by somewhat self-sufficient farmers. The real onset of capitalism occurs with the advent of large-scale industry, which now substantively changes the patterns of life in the countryside.

Chapter 31. The Genesis of the Industrial Capitalist

Unlike the gradual progress of agricultural and manufacturing capitalism, industrial capitalism emerges more quickly, thus typifying the speeding-up of historical change. As we saw in Chapter 4, the Middle Ages produced two proto-capitalist forms: merchant's capital and usurer's capital. But these were 'prevented from turning into industrial capital by the feudal organization of the countryside and the guild organization of the towns' (915). When the rural population was alienated from the lands, 'new manufactures were established at sea-ports, or at points in the countryside which were beyond the control of the old municipalities and their guilds', in order to prevent them from holding back the rise of industrial capital. Notice how capital seeks new spaces that cannot resist its coercive transformation.

The 'chief moments' of the primitive accumulation that ground capitalism, however, do not involve the national theft of land through enclosure, but international theft, with

> the discovery of gold and silver in America, the extirpation, enslavement and entombment in mines of the indigenous population of that continent, the beginnings of the conquest and plunder of India, and the conversion of Africa into a preserve for the commercial hunting of blackskins [slavery],

along with the 'commercial war of the European nations, which has the globe as its battlefield', ranging from Dutch independence to Anglo-French conflicts and colonization. In 'more or less chronological order', the centres of capitalist power over the global market are: 'Spain, Portugal, Holland, France and England' (915). Here are the mutually supporting elements that allow for a quantitative and qualitative shift towards capitalism by the end of the seventeenth century:

> the colonies, the national debt, the modern tax system, and the system of protection. These methods depend in part on brute force, for instance the colonial system. But they all employ the power of the state, the concentrated and organized force of society, to hasten, as in a hothouse, the process of transformation of the feudal mode of production into the capitalist mode, and to shorten the transition. Force is the midwife of every old society which is pregnant with a new one. It is itself an economic power. (915–16)

Marx then recounts the horrors of colonization, through which the 'undisguised looting, enslavement and murder' (918), involving the theft of land and peoples in slavery, provides the capital for European industry. The fruits of imperial aggression stand as the financial source for capitalists to invest in fixed capital that, in turn, will be worked by an exploited national proletariat. Marx repeatedly emphasizes that slavery of non-Europeans only results in worse conditions for the European working-class, as it both creates a latent reserve army of labour that depresses wage demands and provides the capital for machinery that also removes job security.

Public credit and debt also allow for capital to be centralized to large-scale industry. Public debt was necessary to finance colonial adventures to support 'maritime trade and its commercial wars' (919) among European capitalists, for control over global resources. The same is true for international credit systems, where one region's capitalist class is empowered with capital lent by another, as was the case with the United States and Britain throughout the nineteenth century. The state can secure loans based on revenue-generating taxation of the citizenry. Marx argues that overtaxation is a necessary foundation for capitalists, especially tariffs (taxes on the import of non-domestic goods), which help a nation's local industry survive international competition. The cheap labour provided by the colonies and the cheap money from credit allow manufacturers quickly to become large-scale industrialists. In this way, the slavery of the colonies results in the slave-like conditions of the domestic working-class within the factories. Capital comes dripping with blood to make its initial moment of primitive accumulation.

Chapter 32. The Historical Tendency of Capitalist Accumulation

After having described how capitalism began, Marx offers a few words on how he believes it will end. For many readers, this penultimate chapter is a more logical choice to end the volume than the few pages on colonization in the next chapter, which feel slightly misplaced, as if they should appear *before* the present chapter. Here Marx condenses claims that reach their best expression in *The Communist Manifesto*, which he wrote with Friedrich Engels in 1848.

Despite its rise, capitalism also creates 'the material means of its own destruction' (928). Its downfall occurs on two levels. Firstly, there is increased competition among capitalists, who try to outdo one another in the struggle to centralize capital. 'One capitalist always strikes down many others' (929). The tendency towards monopolization is ultimately self-defeating, since capitalism needs competition to force itself to innovate and search for new techniques, regions, and peoples that can be exploited to create more profit. Secondly, and more importantly, capitalists face increasingly fierce class struggle with the 'revolt of the working class, a class constantly increasing in numbers, and trained, unified and organized by the very mechanism of the capitalist process of production' (929). Capitalism's incessant production of the proletariat produces a group that will coalesce to bring it down. Class struggle results in what Marx calls the workers' expropriation of the capitalist class, which has risen by exploiting labourers. If capitalist interests have appropriated public property, then proletarian revolt will turn private property over to communal ownership and construct a modern society that is not based on the search for surplus-value, even if it continues to produce exchangeable commodities.

Chapter 33. The Modern Theory of Colonization

Marx chooses to end the first volume of *Capital* with a note on the colonies, to highlight capitalism's globalizing effects. While the process of primitive accumulation has 'more or less been accomplished' (931) in Western Europe, the same is not true in its colonies. Even if an investor wants to establish capitalist relations elsewhere, these cannot be summoned up merely by the presence of money, since 'capital is not a thing, but a social relation between persons which is mediated through things' (932). One does not need capital, one needs labourers who will be free to be exploited. In the white settler colonies, like Australia or Canada, a class of small proprietors resist the inroads of capitalism by trying to live without commodifying themselves. 'So long, therefore, as the worker can accumulate for himself – and this he can do so long as he remains in possession of his means of production – capitalist accumulation and the capitalist mode of production are impossible' (933). As long as there remains land for immigrants to settle on and farm, then capitalism will have a hard time disciplining workers, especially as they can avoid being proletarianized by making their own goods and living off the produce of their land. These resources allow them to vanish 'from the labour-market but not into the workhouse' (936). This 'anti-capitalist cancer' (938) will continue to prevent the onset of capitalist profiteering until the state puts a price on land that forces colonists to labour for a long time to earn the money to buy property. Even should this happen, immigrants will simply move, looking for ways to escape the labour market. The classic example of this movement is the United States; by the time of *Capital*'s composition, Marx says that capitalism's onset was outpacing even the American West's ability to absorb immigrants and provide land for them to settle. Marx ends the volume by reminding his readers that the fundamental condition for capitalism is that workers are stripped of their freedom of action and pressured to alienate their labour so that capitalists can gain profit. In this light, a post-capitalist society will be one that does not depend on 'the expropriation of the worker' (940).

Suggestions for Further Reading

Introductory Summaries of *Capital*, Vol. I

Anonymous. Capital: *A Readable Introduction to Volume One*, trans. Helen Woggan. London: IMG Publications, 1972.

Brewer, Anthony. *A Guide to Marx's* Capital. Cambridge: Cambridge University Press, 1984.

Cleaver, Harry M. 'Study Guide to *Capital*, vol. I'. <http://www.eco.utexas.edu/faculty/Cleaver/357ksg.html>.

—— *Reading* Capital *Politically*. Austin: University of Texas Press, 1979.

Eldred, Michael and Mike Roth. *Guide to Marx's* Capital. London: CSE Books, 1978.

Engels, Friedrich. 'Synopsis of *Capital*'. 1868. <http://www.marxists.org/archive/marx/works/download/Engels_Synopsis_of_Capital.pdf>.

Fox, John and William Johnston. *Understanding* Capital: *A Guide to Volume I*. Toronto: Progress Books, 1978.

Gellert, Hugo. *Karl Marx's* Capital *in Lithographs*. New York: R. Long & R.R. Smith, 1934. <http://www.graphicwitness.org/contemp/marxtitle.htm>.

Kemp, Tom. *Marx's* Capital *Today*. London: New Park Publications, 1982.

Marx, Karl and Frederick Engels. *Letters on* Capital. Detroit: New Park Publications, 1983.

More Advanced Discussions of Marx's *Capital*

Althusser, Louis and Etienne Balibar. *Reading* Capital, trans. Ben Brewster. London: NLB Books, 1970.

Bidet, Jacques. *Exploring Marx's* Capital: *Philosophical, Economic and Political Dimensions*, trans. David Fernbach. Leiden: Brill, 2007.

Bottomore, Tom (ed.) *A Dictionary of Marxist Thought*. Oxford: Blackwell Reference, 1983.

Dobb, Maurice. *Political Economy and Capitalism*. New York: International Publishers, 1937.

Ehrbar, Hans G. 'Annotations to Marx's *Capital*'. <http://www.econ. utah.edu/~ehrbar/akmc.htm>.

Fine, Ben. *Marx's* Capital. London: Macmillan, 1975.

Harvey, David. *The Limits to Capital*. London: Verso, 1999.

Ito, Makoto. *The Basic Theory of Capitalism: The Forms and Substance of the Capitalist Economy*. Houndmills: Macmillan, 1988.

Mandel, Ernest. *Marxist Economic Theory*. New York: Monthly Review Press, 1968.

McLellan, David. *The Thought of Karl Marx: An Introduction*. London: Macmillan, 1971.

Reiss, Edward. *Marx: A Clear Guide*. London: Pluto Press, 1997.

Rozdolski, Roman. *The Making of Marx's* Capital. London: Pluto Press, 1977.

Wallerstein, Immanuel. *The Modern World-System, vol. I: Capitalist Agriculture and the Origins of the European World-Economy in the Sixteenth Century*. New York: Academic Press, 1974.

English Translations of *Capital*

Marx, Karl. *Capital: A Critique of Political Economy, Volume One*, trans. Ben Fowkes. Harmondsworth: Penguin Books, 1976.

—— *Capital: A Critique of Political Economy, Volume One*, trans. Samuel Moore and Edward Aveling. New York: International Publishers, 1982.

Index

Compiled by Sue Carlton

abstinence theory 148, 149
accidents, industrial 137
accumulation 53, 58, 115, 145–58
  General Law of Capitalist
    Accumulation 150–8
  historical tendencies 171–2
  progressive 149
  reproduction 145–8, 152, 155,
    160
  simple 146, 147–8
  see also primitive (originating)
    accumulation
Age of Handicrafts 99, 116
Age of Large-Scale Machinery
  108, 116, 119
Age of Manufacture 12, 99, 105,
  118, 119, 122, 129, 160
agriculture
  agricultural revolution 138,
    167–8
  and capitalist appropriation
    158
alienation 33, 41, 49, 58, 64, 65,
  101, 125
apprentices 94, 99, 110, 113
Aristotle 27, 35
artificial intelligence 120
assembly line 109
automaton 121, 128

barter 23, 49, 69
basic needs 66, 76, 125, 147

Bentham, Jeremy 69, 150
Black Death 162
business cycle 151–2

capital
  centralization of 152–3, 170,
    171
  constant 78–9, 80, 100, 123,
    149, 151, 153
  definition of 55, 58
  organic composition of 150–1
  as part of social wealth 149–50
  variable 79, 80, 123, 151, 153
  see also General Formula for
    Capital
capital-relation 130, 140, 146, 160
capitalism
  definition of 68, 71
  and disempowerment of
    workers 68–9
  emergence of 4, 157, 159–62
    see also primitive
      (originating) accumulation
  global 39, 50, 137, 158, 172
  and international theft 169–70
  and need for social
    transformation 138–9
  originating in violence 159–60
capitalists
  capitalist farmers 167
  industrial 168–70

Catholic Church, dissolution of 163–4, 165
centralization 152–3, 170, 171
Chartist movement 90
child workers
    and machine operation 124–6, 129
    working day 88, 89
circulation 43–54
    means of 46–52
        see also money
    velocity of (liquidity) 51–2, 59
class relations, maintenance and reproduction of 146–7, 150, 155, 171
class struggle 85, 126, 130, 131, 145, 171
class system 159
clearing of estates, Scotland 165–6
co-operation 98–105
colonies, and resistance to capitalism 172–3
colonization 169–70, 172–3
commodities
    and abstract value 24, 25–7, 28, 32–4
    circulation of 46–52
    definition of 6–7, 15, 19, 72–3
    and value 7–10
commodity chain 50, 54
commodity exchange 33, 49, 69
commodity fetishism 32–40, 59, 101
commodity-form 33, 39
common land 162, 163, 165
compensation theory 132, 133–4
competition 48, 93, 153, 170, 171
constant capital 78–9, 80, 100, 123, 149, 151, 153

contracts 146–7
copper coinage 44
cotton 87, 124, 135, 166
credit 42, 52, 54, 153, 170
cycle of trade 51, 59, 137, 146
C–M–C (commodity–money–commodity) circuit 47–8, 50, 57

deskilling 107, 110–11, 113, 125
division of labour 17–19, 21, 25, 32–3, 105–7, 129
    and forms of manufacture 108–11
    impact on worker 106–7, 114
    international 135
    social 17–18, 21, 32–3, 105–7, 111–13, 129

education/training 20, 77, 110, 114, 126
enclosure 163
Engels, Friedrich 80, 171
England
    and expropriation of farmers 161–6
    wool production 163, 166
English Factory Legislation (1833–64) 89–90, 137–8
exchange, process of 40–3
exchange-value 7–16, 18–20, 21–31, 32–3, 75
    and commodity fetishism 32–3, 35, 38, 39
    and money 43, 46, 48, 50, 52, 56, 57–8
    and surplus-value 58, 61, 63, 68, 98, 148
expanded form of value 29–30

exploitation 71, 72, 81–2, 137–8, 146, 150, 167
  and division of labour 114
  and length of working day 82–3, 84, 88–9, 92
  and technology 118

factory 128–30
  definition of 128
Factory Acts *see* English Factory Legislation
farmers
  expropriation from land 161–6
  as original capitalists 167
feudalism 38, 104, 161, 162–3, 169
Fourier, Charles 130
France, Anatole 70
free trade 1–2, 28, 90, 165

general form of value 30–1
General Formula for Capital 55–9, 150
  contradictions in 60–3
General Law of Capitalist Accumulation 150–8
  illustrations of 157–8
Glorious Revolution (1688) 164
gold and silver 30–1, 42, 43, 51, 87, 169
  gold reserves 28, 52
guilds 94, 107–8, 113, 161

ideas/perceptions, and social formation 27–8, 36–7
individuality 40, 101
industrial revolution 115, 119
inflation 50–1, 167
  causes of 51
  and profit 62
interest 45, 62

internet 74
invisible hand 2
Ireland 158

job creation 133–4

labour
  co-operation 98–105
  creation of value 11–16, 51, 64
    see also labour theory of value
  dual character of 16–22
  increasing productivity 98
  mental and manual division 94, 102, 106, 111
  oversupply of 51
  skilled and unskilled 20, 77, 110, 113, 129
  and surplus value 73
    see also surplus-value, and labour-power
  unpaid 73, 77, 80, 94–5, 141, 152
labour fund 149–50
labour process 72–5
  instruments of labour 73, 74–5, 76, 78, 80–1, 91
    see also machinery
  object of the work (nature) 73–4
  and raw materials 74, 76, 78, 79
  work (human purposeful activity) 73
labour theory of value 12
  see also labour, creation of value
labour-power 20, 25
  definition of 64
  determining value of 66–7

and mode of production 96–7
replaced by machinery 123–4,
    128
sale and purchase of 63–71
and surplus-value 64, 67, 70,
    76–7, 79, 98, 128, 151–2
and wages 142–3, 151, 152
labour-time 12–14, 37, 86
average 99
as measure of value 14, 19–20,
    21, 40, 43, 44, 60, 66, 67
reducing 96–7
and wages 76–7
see also working day
labourers/workers
conditions for selling labour-
    power 64–5
disempowerment of 68–9
and freedom 64–6, 68–70, 75
interaction with nature 73–4
lack of rights 166–7
resisting capitalism 131
and solidarity 102–3, 110, 126
working and living conditions
    88–90, 126–7, 136–7,
    157–8
land/property 42, 56–7
large-scale industry 117–39
impact on rural life 168
machinery and tools
    distinction 118–20, 121,
    122
see also factory, machinery
Le Chapelier Law 167
liquidity 51–2
loans, and interest 45, 62
long-distance merchants, and
    profit 62–3
Luddites 130–1
luxuries 134, 149

machinery 13–14, 80, 81, 115,
    117–39, 143
and artificial intelligence 120
and capitalist expansion and
    contraction 134–6
complex system of 120–2
constant operation of 89, 127
definition of 119
and depreciation 127
development of 117–23
as distinct from tools 118–20,
    121, 122
effects on workers and families
    124–8, 129–30, 136–7
erasing job hierarchies 129
investment in 78, 94, 153
and overproduction 136
and reduction in wages 132
reliance on 153–4
and suppression of strikes 133
and unemployment 132, 133–4
and value transfer 78–9, 123–4
worker's struggle with 130–3
see also new technologies
Malthus, Thomas 150, 154
manufacture 105–11
capitalist character of 113–17
heterogeneous 108–9
organic 109
see also Age of Manufacture
market place, and freedom and
    equality 69–70, 85
market-fetish 59
material wealth 8, 22
means of production 39, 65, 68,
    74, 78–9, 91, 151
commons 162
ownership of 66, 86, 160, 172
Mercantilists, and hoarding 28,
    52

Mill, John Stuart 150
mode of production 27, 53, 65, 66, 74, 87, 154
  and accumulation 154, 160, 169, 172
  labour co-operation 98–105
  revolutions in 91, 96–7, 115, 117, 120, 122
  and surplus-value 91, 92, 96–7, 151
money 30–3, 37, 40–54
  definition of 43
  hoarding 52–4, 58–9
  as means of circulation 46–52
  as measure of value 43, 44, 45–6, 53
  as standard of price 43–6, 50
  as symbolic form 42–3
  transformation into capital 55–71
money fetish 43, 49, 59
money-form 23, 30–1, 33, 41, 45–6, 52, 55, 142
monopolization 152, 171
M–C–M circuit 57–8, 59, 147

necessary labour 66, 80, 81, 83, 93, 97, 125
needs 6–7, 13
  basic needs 66, 76, 125, 147
  subsistence needs 66–7
  use needs 17–18, 24–5, 66
new technologies
  and commodity value 13–14
  demand for raw materials 135
  invention and use 120
  and profit 128, 171
  workers and 129, 130–1, 133
  and working day 91, 117–18
  see also machinery

overtime 143
overwork 84, 90, 99, 114, 118, 127
  forced labour 87, 89
  limit to 95, 98, 115
  and technological advances 91, 118

paper money 44, 51–2
pauperism 155–6, 164, 165, 166
piece-wages 144
pre-capitalist societies
  and labour co-operation 104–5
  and surplus labour 86–7
price 31, 34, 35, 43–8, 50–1, 53, 55, 143
  of labour 64, 67, 68, 69, 70–1, 76–7, 93, 132, 141
  see also wages
  and value 44–6, 60, 62
  see also inflation
price-form 29, 44, 45
primitive (originating) accumulation 157, 159–73
  and expropriation of farmers from land 161–6
  genesis of capitalist farmer 167
  genesis of industrial capitalist 168–70
  secret of 159–62
  and violence 159–60
production, and efficiency 13, 84, 94, 101–2, 108, 152
profit 2, 38, 56, 57–8, 59
  rate of 80, 98
  sources of 60–3, 68, 70, 71
proletariat
  definition of proletarian 65, 151
  production of 152, 161, 162–3, 165, 171

How to Read Marx's *Capital*

proletarian identity 138
proletarian revolt 171–2

raw materials
 and demand of new
 technologies 135
 and labour process 74, 76, 78,
 79
relative surplus population
 different forms of 155–7
 progressive production of
 153–5
reproduction 145–8, 152, 155, 160
 simple 146, 147–8
Robinson Crusoe 37–8
rural workers
 effects of capitalism on 68–9,
 131–2, 138
 moving to cities 167–8

Scotland, expropriation of farmers
 from land 165–6
Scott, Walter 165–6
Senior, Nassau 82
serfdom 38, 64–5, 68–9, 86, 87,
 161, 162
service sector 133, 134
simple form of value 23–9
slavery 86, 87–8, 89, 90, 91, 104,
 170
Smith, Adam 1–2, 3–4, 19, 114,
 141, 143, 164–5
social division of labour 17–18,
 21, 32–3, 105–7, 111–13, 129
socialism 3, 68
specialization 106, 107–8
 and hierarchy of jobs 110, 113
 and machinery 122–3
 and tools 108, 110
stock market 28–9, 59

strikes, impact of machinery 122,
 131, 133
subsistence needs 66–7
supply and demand 143, 152,
 153–4
surplus labour 80, 81, 82, 83,
 86–7, 93, 152
surplus-value 58, 59, 60–3
 absolute and relative 83, 92–3,
 95, 96–8, 127, 140–1, 151,
 166
 and cheating 61, 62, 70, 95
 creating 75–7
 from efficiency 94, 101–2
 from new machinery 93–4
 and intensity of labour 141,
 142
 and labour co-operation 98–105
 and labour-power 64, 67, 70,
 76–7, 79, 98, 128, 151–2
 and length of working day
 83–5, 92, 93, 96, 98, 141,
 142, 143
 and productivity of labour 141,
 142
 rate of 79–82, 92, 93, 141
 transformation into capital
 147–50
sweating system 144

tariffs 2, 28, 90, 170
taxation 2, 169, 170
trade 2, 10, 17–19, 35, 47–8, 56
 cycle of 51, 59, 137, 146
 expanding boundaries 49–50,
 54
 long-distance 55, 62
trade relations, historical origins
 of 39–40, 41–2
trade unions 122, 138, 166

unemployment 152, 154–5
  and compensation theory 132,
    133–4
  increasing competition 151,
    152, 154
  industrial reserve army 137,
    154, 156
United States
  and immigration 173
  and public debt 170
  working day 91
use needs 17–18, 24, 66
use-value 7–8, 10–11, 13–19,
    21–2, 24–5, 45–7, 53
  gold and silver 31, 43
  and socialism 68
  and surplus-value 58, 75, 96, 140
usurers, and profit 62–3, 168
utilitarians 69, 150

valorization process 75–7
value-form 21, 22–31
  expanded form of value 29–30
  general form of value 30–1
  scientific metaphor 23–4
  simple form of value 23–9
variable capital 79, 80, 123, 151,
    153

wages 66, 69, 93, 108, 114, 142–4
  and contracts 146–7

and division of labour 110–11
impact of machinery 130, 132
national differences 144
regulating 90, 166
and value of labour-power 79,
  142–3, 151, 152
see also price, of labour
Walkley, Mary Anne 89
Welfare State 155
Whitney, Eli 124
William of Orange 164
women
  impact of capitalism 139
  and machine operation 124–6
wool manufacture 163, 166
worker combinations 166–7
workers see labourers/workers
working day 82–92
  child workers 88, 89
  and increasing surplus-value
    83–5, 92, 93, 96, 98
  laws for compulsory extension
    of 89
  laws for compulsory limitation
    of 89–90
  and life expectancy 88–9
  limits of 83–5, 98
  and machinery 127–8
  overwork 87
  shift-system 89
  United States 91